Benedict Collins is a political journalist working for *1News* in the press gallery in Wellington. From his first days as a reporter, he's had a strong interest in covering anything to do with illicit drugs and enforcement. He's covered punitive drug-testing sanctions applied to beneficiaries, attempts to legalise pill-testing at festivals, the 2020 cannabis referendum, and in 2018, helped expose a meth-testing scandal that had government, landlords and homeowners wasting hundreds of millions of dollars.

MAD ON METH

BENEDICT COLLINS

HarperCollins*Publishers*

HarperCollins*Publishers*
Australia • Brazil • Canada • France • Germany • Holland • India
Italy • Japan • Mexico • New Zealand • Poland • Spain • Sweden
Switzerland • United Kingdom • United States of America

First published in 2023
by HarperCollins*Publishers* (New Zealand) Limited
Unit D1, 63 Apollo Drive, Rosedale, Auckland 0632, New Zealand
harpercollins.co.nz

Copyright © Benedict Collins 2023

Benedict Collins asserts the moral right to be identified as the author of this work. This work is copyright. All rights reserved. No part of this publication may be reproduced, copied, scanned, stored in a retrieval system, recorded, or transmitted, in any form or by any means, without the prior written permission of the publisher.

A catalogue record for this book is available from the National Library of New Zealand

ISBN 978 1 7755 4200 1 (paperback)
ISBN 978 1 7754 9231 3 (ebook)

Cover design by Michelle Zaiter, HarperCollins Design Studio
Cover images by istockphoto.com
Author photograph by Sam Anderson
Photographs are public domain or courtesy of the author's collection unless otherwise specified
Typeset in Adobe Garamond Pro by Kirby Jones
Printed and bound in Australia by McPherson's Printing Group

For Claire, Skye and Maisie.

CONTENTS

	Introduction	1
1	'We Ride on Dynamite'	9
2	Amphetamines: 'A Boon to Mankind'	29
3	'Spawn of the Devil'	44
4	Hungry for Business	61
5	Crystal Meth Academy	77
6	Moral Panic	92
7	Dread Pirate Roberts	111
8	White-collar 'Chemical Man'	130
9	'Horrible, Horrible Man'	146
10	Zombieland	158
11	Straight Shooting	178
12	The 'Most Sneakiest' Drug in the World	196
13	'Havoc, Harm and Upheaval'	211
14	The Punisher	226
15	Frankenstein: Breaking the Cycle	246
	Further Reading	258
	Acknowledgements	263

INTRODUCTION

IT WAS NEWS I REALLY DIDN'T NEED TO HEAR. 'HI BENEDICT, I would like to disclose that the meth samples taken came back positive, so you are fully aware.'

I'd been on a run of bad luck lately. It was early 2017 and my Lyall Bay flat in Wellington had just been burgled, leaving me sitting in my lounge sans TV and MacBook after work each night with only my transistor radio for entertainment. The following week I'd spent five minutes unsuccessfully trying to reverse my car out of the carport and onto the street on a pitch-black winter's night, and while the engine revved and revved the car didn't budge. Despite my lack of know-how, I popped the bonnet and got out to investigate, but before I even made it to the front of the car I had diagnosed the fault. My station-wagon was sitting on piles of small wooden blocks – its four mag wheels that had been there that morning were gone, meeting the same destiny as my laptop and TV.

The universe was sending me a message: it was time to get out of that flat. So when I came across a just-affordable two-and-a-half-bedroom ex-state house for sale in Cannons Creek, Porirua, on Trade Me, I was almighty keen to put in a bid.

It was freshly repainted, the kitchen and bathroom recently renovated, and the real estate agent let me know that a previously accepted offer on the home had only just fallen through. I contacted a builder to purchase the building report he'd done for the former prospective buyers and, when he asked if I also wanted to purchase the results of the meth testing he'd carried out on the home, I began to get a hunch as to why the former buyers had suddenly pulled out of the deal.

At the time I was working as a journalist at Radio New Zealand and had been investigating the meth-testing industry, airing the concerns of scientists and other experts who were convinced meth testing was nothing but a complete and utter scam. Nevertheless, there were also those who believed traces of methamphetamine posed an immense threat to people's health – particularly in houses that were used to cook the drug. There was no disputing the fact that homes all over the country were being decontaminated at huge expense and in some cases even destroyed because of methamphetamine contamination. Everywhere you turned there were dire warnings about the dangers of meth contamination, from our politicians, officials, the press, and especially from those who were carrying out the testing.

I had a dilemma on my hands: pay for meth testing which I strongly suspected was a con, or pay up and learn whether I really was about to buy a meth-contaminated house.

After a stern warning from a fellow reporter to not dare pay for it, I emailed the builder declining the results of this meth test – to which he promptly sent the response warning me that the house had tested positive. But he also told me that his tests were so rudimentary he had no way of telling what level of meth there actually was in the home, nor whether those traces of this illegal drug were above or below the health authority's controversial testing guidelines.

If I wanted to have a more accurate picture, the builder said, I'd have to pay for a specialist meth-testing company to come in and carry out more advanced, and much more expensive, testing at the property. That was something I simply couldn't swallow.

There was no suggestion the property had ever been a meth lab so, with a little trepidation, I signed on the dotted line. Perhaps ironically, the public's fear around meth testing had just helped me get a foot on the property ladder. Yet still I applied sugar soap liberally to the walls and surfaces after taking the keys, just to be sure.

I was one of a vast number of New Zealanders who got caught up in needless widespread testing for methamphetamine, consumed by a fear of what even the most minuscule trace could do — even to people who had nothing to do with the drug itself.

* * *

How did we end up here? A little over 20 years ago, armed with online and word-of-mouth recipes, hundreds of amateur Kiwi 'chemists' began trying their hand at cooking meth in makeshift labs in homes, on farms and at commercial premises. Seemingly out of nowhere, this illegal drug had become a key commodity in the underworld. The cooks found that by mixing a little pseudoephedrine, sourced from a packet of cold and flu medicine from their local pharmacy, with a handful of additional chemicals, they could recreate the century-old recipe for the powerful central nervous stimulant, methamphetamine.

And P was proving to be pretty popular with the public, with tens of thousands of New Zealanders soon sampling this crystallised rocket fuel. Why wouldn't they? A good hit of methamphetamine sends your heart rate and energy levels soaring: you're more awake and focused, your senses are heightened and mass amounts of dopamine start firing around in your brain – you're absolutely amped.

Got chores to do? No problem. Want to party? Bring it on.

But as more and more people began experimenting with P, it wasn't long before cases of full-blown addiction and reports of meth-related crime escalated. New Zealand politicians retaliated, following the lead of other nations, by cracking down on the sale of pseudoephedrine. However, while this was well-meaning, cracking down on the domestic manufacturing of P inadvertently turbo-charged the meth trade, because it didn't take long for warlords, triads and cartels around the world to spot a lucrative opening in the drug market.

In the last 15 years or so, there's been an avalanche of P cooked and trafficked and dumped on the world. In 2021, a record 393 tonnes of meth were seized by authorities, globally, and if that's just the amount intercepted, you can safely assume many more thousands of tonnes of it is being consumed. That 2021 haul was well over five times more meth than law enforcement had seized a decade earlier, and if you wind the calendar back to 1998, just a couple of tonnes of meth was seized in total around the world. The international meth trade is growing exponentially.

If you're into making and trafficking illegal drugs, it just doesn't get much better than meth. The return on investment is simply incredible. Not only is it fast and cheap to make, but you've also got between 30 and 50 million customers out there, a good number of them becoming steadily hooked on your product. You can swamp regions with cheap meth like they're doing in South-east Asia and reserve your top-quality crystal meth for your wealthier clients in New Zealand and Australia.

Synthetic drugs like meth are a godsend to criminal groups – they're just so much less hassle than plant-based drugs like cocaine or heroin. With meth, there's no need for growers, so you don't have to go through the rigmarole of planting crops or providing security to ensure they're protected and safe until you harvest. All you need to make quality meth is a chemist and lots and lots of chemicals. You're not reliant on the seasons or the soil, there's no battling the weather or pests, and you're nowhere near as visible to the authorities in a clandestine meth lab compared with hectares of illegal crops out in the open.

Another big advantage of manufacturing P, from an organised crime perspective, is that recipes can easily be tweaked – you can substitute chemicals in and out at any point along the chain. Also, should one of your shipments get busted by authorities, sure it's an inconvenience, but in the bigger scheme of things, it's kind of irrelevant, because you can cook up another batch tomorrow. The speed and ease with which it can be made means having your meth seized just isn't as big a blow as them seizing your blow.

Nowadays, most of New Zealand's P is manufactured in super labs in Myanmar and to a lesser extent Mexico. At a minimum hundreds and hundreds of kilos of high-quality meth is now being sent here every year. Much of the importation and distribution of it is controlled by the underworld, a mix of well-connected Asian criminal organisations and some gangs, both equally attracted to the immense profits that can be made trading meth.

As we've seen over the last 25 years, when some of the most ruthless members of society control the supply of a powerful and addictive drug like meth, it creates the perfect conditions for maximising harm and carnage in our communities.

But meth didn't just arrive out of the blue on our shores in the late 1990s. It had been used here legally by thousands of New Zealanders – along with other similar and now forbidden stimulants – decades earlier, and often without too much of a fuss. So that is what this book explores – the evolution of the drug we now know as P.

As a journalist who'd investigated the hysteria around meth testing, the opportunity to take this deep dive into the nation's most feared drug was one I just couldn't pass up. I've interviewed those in charge of the global fight against meth who concede that many governments are now at a loss over what to do, and families in small-town New Zealand whose lives have been turned upside down by a loved one's meth addiction.

I delve into specific cases over the years that helped cement methamphetamine's notorious reputation and which illustrate the catastrophic outcomes of dangerous people out of control on meth, people like Coral Ellen Burrows's stepdad, and samurai-sword attacker Antoine Dixon. And I talk to heavy users who don't think meth's as bad as it's made out to be. Ultimately I trace and evaluate the success of the strategies of governments here in New Zealand who have tried to pull every lever they have to combat P, and I question whether there's a better way to get on top of the meth problem.

What's the full story about meth? Well, let's find out.

CHAPTER 1
'WE RIDE ON DYNAMITE'
Meth and Its Many Uses from War to Sports

THE KIWI TROOPS COULDN'T BELIEVE THEIR EYES, OR THEIR luck, as waves of German troops, who were frothing at the mouth and screaming, with their arms linked, charged recklessly at the ANZAC's fortified positions around Mount Olympus in April 1941. Company after company of drug-crazed soldiers were blown to pieces as they ran straight into the blazing muzzles of the Aussie and Kiwi guns, and even as they dropped like flies, the Germans just kept on coming, with apparently zero regard for their lives.

And if that wasn't bizarre enough, the Nazi corpses quickly turned green.

This was the story that those picking up a copy of their local paper in Manawatū were greeted with on 19 June 1941, the article, headlined 'Yelled Like Maniacs', recounted the experience of a New Zealand soldier, who had recently landed in Sydney on his way back home after fighting the Germans in Greece. 'The Nazis were clearly doped to the eyeballs,' he recalled, and their suicidal behaviour must have been the result of being under the influence of a very powerful drug indeed.

A chemist, who was also interviewed for the article, suggested the drug may have been Methedrine, which, he said, can produce intense stimulation, bucketloads of self-confidence, quick thinking, a loss of fear, and restlessness. And in hot climates, the chemist confirmed, the corpses of those doped would certainly turn black and then green.

So why do I bring up this report about hundreds of frothy mouthed suicidal soldiers? It might sound far-fetched, or just wartime propaganda, but there's no doubt German troops were consuming methamphetamine by the tonne during the Second World War.

When German paratroopers jumped out of their planes high above Crete on 20 May 1941, directly above a battalion of New Zealand troops who were just finishing up their breakfast, they must have seemed like they had a death wish, too, as the first 100 to 150 German paratroopers were dead before they hit the ground, while one poor Jerry who floated down directly above the platoon kicked and writhed in his harness as he was turned into Swiss cheese by bullets before landing with a thud. It reminded 2nd Lieutenant Buck Taylor of duck-shooting season back home. But the enemy kept coming and soon enough Taylor himself had been shot in the hand.

As he returned to New Zealand, he brought back a number of items including a 1942 British intelligence report that detailed the disastrous Battle of Crete. His son, military history enthusiast retired Major Noel Taylor, sent me part of the report that had been produced by Britain's War Office and distributed to New Zealand officers with this instruction on the front page: THIS DOCUMENT MUST NOT FALL INTO ENEMY HANDS. It was Britain's assessment of how the German paratroopers had operated in the battle, in which approximately 670 Kiwi troops were killed and 2000 more taken as prisoners of war.

The first German paratroopers to land were armed with a large jack-knife, four grenades and an automatic pistol with two magazines, while every fourth paratrooper carried a submachine gun strapped to their back. But the report also said that the soldiers were fuelled by drugs, that they used Pervitin, 'a drug allied to Benzedrine, to produce wakefulness and alertness … and is said to make one thirsty'. Pervitin was another brand name for methamphetamine. In addition to securing a camera and a Luger pistol from a dead paratrooper, Lt Taylor brought home a container of pills, which family legend had always believed were Nazi meth pills, but on closer examination turned out to be less illicit Vitamin-A-infused Nazi sweets.

* * *

German scientists at a pharmaceutical company, Temmler, had become interested in Benzedrine after it was used, legally, by athletes to boost their performances at the 1936 Olympics in Berlin and they decided to research this. A Romanian chemist of Jewish origin, Lazăr Edeleanu, had written a paper about how he had synthesised amphetamine, while working at the University of Berlin in 1887, although he became much more famous for figuring out how to refine crude oil. Not much happened with amphetamine for another 40 years until it was realised that the drug mimics our brain's natural stimulant, norepinephrine, which is released in huge amounts when we're stressed or in danger, and boosts our alertness, vigilance and focuses our attention. It also spikes our heart rate and blood pressure, and opens our airways.

Amphetamine was initially used to treat narcolepsy (a sleep disorder characterised by extreme tiredness and sudden sleep attacks during the day). As it also affects the airways, it was then sold as a nasal decongestant and marketed as Benzedrine from the mid-1930s. But the scientists at Temmler were more interested in a similar but more powerful stimulant, methamphetamine, the origins of which can be traced back to a chance discovery made in 1885 at the Tokyo Imperial University. A Japanese chemist, Nagayoshi Nagai, and his team were experimenting with traditional medicinal herbs, trying to unlock and understand the secrets behind their healing properties, when a colleague crushed up a sample of ma huang and noticed that there were tiny fine crystals present in the paste. Ma huang is a plant that had been brewed in tea for thousands of years across Asia, used to help alleviate the symptoms of the common cold. In the West the plant is known as ephedra.

Professor Nagayoshi, who had only recently returned from Berlin where he too had studied how to synthesise chemicals for medicinal purposes, began to experiment with ma huang, and two years later he isolated the stimulant ephedrine from the plant. It didn't take long before ephedrine was on the market as a bronchodilator drug – one which widens the throat and airways – making it easier for people with colds, flus or asthma to breathe, and has been used in medicines ever since.

But Nagayoshi didn't stop there, continuing to experiment with ephedrine until in 1893 he synthesised a substance he called methamphetamine. At the time, he felt it didn't appear to have any beneficial properties for humans, so the recipe for meth sat on the shelf for the next few decades. Then in 1919, Professor Nagayoshi's apprentice Ogata Akira went a step further when he reduced ephedrine with red phosphorus and iodine and produced methamphetamine hydrochloride. Observing the tiny crystals in front of him, he couldn't have known he had just made the most powerful stimulant on the planet.

Crystal meth was born.

When Professor Nagayoshi became the first president of Japan's distinguished Pharmaceutical Society he issued this advice to his fellow chemists: 'Invent medicines that can be easily absorbed by the body through research on natural medicine and chemical synthesis. Then let's introduce Japanese pharmaceutical sciences to the world.'

By 1937, the scientists at Temmler did just that. They'd done their homework on crystal methamphetamine and explored new ways of making it and on 31 October that year they patented Pervitin; Benzedrine on steroids. The following year, posters for Pervitin, advertising that it could reverse low energy and depression and even frigidity in women, were plastered on the walls at train stations and at tram stops across Berlin. German doctors were being sent three free pills in sample packs by Temmler, which wanted to receive feedback regarding their experiences taking the drug, and soon citizens were purchasing hundreds of Pervitin pills at a time when they visited the chemist.

Not only was Pervitin marketed as something that could help boost your confidence or give a little pick-me-up before a party or performance but they were also advertised to help make household chores a lot less tedious. Boxes of Hildebrand's chocolates, containing 14 milligrams of methamphetamine per chocolate (three times the dose of a Pervitin pill), were marketed to German housewives. 'Hildebrand chocolates, always a delight' the packaging read.

But it was the Nazi military that really seized upon methamphetamine's fatigue-fighting properties and used it to chemically fuel their troops, so they could fight for days without rest and their pilots could stay alert on long bombing missions. In his 2017 book, *Blitzed: Drugs in Nazi Germany*, the writer Norman Ohler details how, following the Olympics, the Third Reich's top defence physiologist Otto Ranke carried out experiments on about 150 army medical officers with different stimulants – Pervitin, Benzedrine, coffee or a placebo – keeping them up through the night solving maths equations. By the following morning, those who had been given the placebo were propping up their heads on their hands at the desks while those who had taken Pervitin were still beavering away at their sums. Although they were wide awake, it actually didn't make them any smarter as their calculations contained more mistakes, nevertheless Ranke concluded that Pervitin was 'an excellent substance for rousing a weary squad' and that methamphetamine could have far-reaching military significance.

The recommended dose of Pervitin had the added bonus of being about a third of the price of coffee, and so the German military began buying vast quantities of Pervitin to turbocharge their forces. An order was placed with Temmler for 35 million Pervitin pills; the factory pumped out more than 800,000 methamphetamine tablets a day. German soldiers on the frontlines wrote home asking to be sent more Pervitin, while one pilot wrote of their experience after taking three tablets while flying above the Mediterranean:

> The engine is running cleanly and calmly. I'm wide awake, my heartbeat thunders in my ears. When the sky is suddenly so bright, my eyes hurt from the harsh light. I can hardly hear the brilliance: if I shield my eyes with my free hand it's better. Now the engine is humming evenly and without vibration far away, very far away. It's almost like silence up here. Everything becomes immaterial and abstract. Remote, as if I were flying above my plane.

Ohler also records how thousands of German troops took the prescribed Pervitin as they launched their blitzkrieg across swathes of Europe, racing their tanks, troops and artillery through the Ardennes Forest and into Belgium, the speed of their offensive catching defending soldiers off-guard. The German military went days without sleep, allowing them to overrun Belgium, France and then much of Europe.

As for Adolf Hitler, the chants of Heil Hitler (health to Hitler) didn't bear fruit. Ohler describes him as a super-junkie, who for years would be given daily injections of vitamins, animal tonics and towards the end of the war (and his life) cocaine, opioids and on at least one occasion an injection of liver and Pervitin.

But it wasn't just their own medical officers that the Germans carried out meth experiments on. At the Sachsenhausen concentration camp, north of Berlin, which was opened the same year as the 1936 Olympics, there was a walking unit, in which the prisoners, a combination of roma, homosexuals, political prisoners and some Jews, were forced to walk kilometres a day, week after week, around a 700-metre track in order to test the best footwear for German troops. Carrying heavy packs, prisoners often walked until they collapsed, at which point if they were still alive, they would be set upon by an Alsatian dog.

By November 1944, prisoners were also used to test the effectiveness of high doses of cocaine and Pervitin and made to march through the night, coined the 'pill patrol'. It's been said they walked and whistled through the night; a 20-year-old inmate who had been given 75 milligrams of cocaine walked 96 kilometres without stopping. In Germany's *Focus* magazine, in 2002, a former prisoner was interviewed and recalled that they were also given a drug codenamed D-IX – a potent mix of cocaine, methamphetamine and eukodol (oxycodone) – that the military was hoping would give soldiers 'unlimited fighting powers', but the war ended before it was rolled out en masse.

Second World War Japanese soldiers and wartime workers were also liberally issued with meth, under the brand names Philopon or Hiripon, known as 'the drug to inspire a fighting spirit'. At the conclusion of the war, Japan's unused methamphetamine stockpiles quickly made their way into the communities of a country humiliatingly defeated in the war and now in the midst of a severe economic depression. So much so that by the mid-1950s, Japan was estimated to have 1.5 million meth users, in a country of 88 million.

British and American troops were also given vast quantities of Benzedrine in North Africa in 1942 – but it was in Vietnam where amphetamine use rocketed.

* * *

According to a report by the United States House Select Committee on Crime in 1971, the Pentagon issued more than 200 million stimulant pills to troops between 1966 and 1969 in the Vietnam War, mainly Dexedrine, an amphetamine almost twice the strength of Benzedrine.

In *Shooting Up: A History of Drugs in Warfare*, Lukasz Kamieński quotes Elton Manzione, who had been the commander of a long-range reconnaissance platoon in Vietnam as saying 'we had the best amphetamines available and they were supplied by the US Government'. Another soldier recalled how Dexedrine not only kept them awake but also gave them a sense of bravado, every sight and sound was heightened, they were extremely alert, they felt invincible.

And the use of amphetamines in the US military continues, with fighter and bomber pilots known to have been handed Dexedrine tablets ('go' pills), before takeoff by medical staff during the 2001–2021 US war in Afghanistan, to help them stay alert and focused during long missions; when they landed, they were issued sleeping tablets ('no go' pills) to knock them out.

The US Air Force assistant Surgeon General, and former fighter pilot, Colonel Pete Demitry describes Dexedrine as an insurance policy against fatigue for pilots, while a Gulf War commander laughed off concerns about pilots flying high on amphetamines: 'If you can't trust them with the medication, then you can't trust them with a $50 million airplane to try and go kill someone.'

Two American F-16 fighter pilots who were on Dexedrine and flying a night mission above Khandahar in 2003 thought they had come under fire from Taliban fighters and promptly dropped a 500-pound laser-guided bomb. But it turned out the Taliban fighters were actually Canadian soldiers who were carrying out a night-training mission at a former al-Qaeda training camp. Four soldiers were killed and eight more injured. They were the first Canadian combat deaths since the Korean War. Charged for the friendly-fire deaths and their poor airmanship, the pilots argued they had been forced by the US Air Force to take their go pills, which had impaired their judgement. Their lawyer argued that the air force had never explained the potential side effects of Dexedrine, and pointed out the label on the GlaxoSmithKline drug made it clear that using the drug could impair people's ability to operate vehicles and machinery, which obviously included fighter jets.

In response, the air force said it had never had a report of Dexedrine contributing to an accident, whereas fatigue had contributed to around 100 accidents. One of the pilots promptly retired while the other eventually had charges dropped against him.

Commenting on the use of stimulants, a US Navy officer told *The LA Times* that, in comparison, very few navy pilots took amphetamines, partly due to their much shorter flights and also, he said, would you really want to be landing on an aircraft carrier at night while on amphetamines?

* * *

Athletes have been taking amphetamines to boost alertness, endurance and performance for the best part of a century, as they sought to break through barriers and excel in their fields.

Covering the Tour de France for *Sports Illustrated* in 1966, the American journalist Jack Olsen wrote of rampant amphetamine use among the riders and concluded the tour was not just a bike race.

'Who ever heard of a bike race that lasts three weeks and features a dozen dozen athletes fetchingly attired in advertising messages front and derriere, cycling their hearts out, with the help of a load of Dexedrine that would stagger even the students at NYU and Berkeley?' he wrote.

And as for the Lanterne Rouge, or Red Lantern, the last-placed rider in the tour, Olsen wrote: 'He may have lost his toenails from the constant forward pressure in his cycling shoes … and his mind so addled by amphetamine that he is not sure of his name, but he is a hero, a major athletic figure, a finisher in the Tour de France, the most trying sports event on earth'.

Clearly, not much attention was being paid to the American Medical Association, which a year earlier had claimed these amphetamine and meth pills, which had become collectively known as pep pills, contributed no more to athletic success than the superstition of never changing your underwear while on a winning streak.

The cyclists knew better. The use of drugs was so endemic on the tour, the sporting editor of the French newspaper *Le Figaro* wrote that while all the riders were on dope, they took dope intelligently and were 15 years ahead of athletes in other sports. Riding on the tour was so demanding, he argued, they had to take something. 'There is no other event in the world where you have to keep going in a maximum effort six hours a day for 22 days. It just cannot be done without dope.'

On 13 July 1967, the great British rider Tommy Simpson collapsed a kilometre from the summit while climbing Mont Ventoux on a blistering hot day. Despite attempts at resuscitation on the roadside and being flown in a police helicopter to nearby Avignon Hospital, he died that night. Two empty vials of methamphetamine and another half full were found on him as well as brandy in his water bottle. Britain's *Daily Mail* reported that Simpson had ridden to his death so doped up he didn't realise he'd reached the limit of his endurance. 'He died in the saddle, slowly asphyxiated by intense effort in a heatwave after taking methylamphetamine drugs and alcoholic stimulants forbidden by French law,' the story read (although stiff penalties for amphetamine use on the tour had only been in place for a year).

Stimulants had been widely used by riders on the tour for decades. More than 40 years earlier, in 1924, a reporter, Albert Londres, was covering the race for the daily paper *Le Petit Parisien* when he came up with one of the biggest journalistic scoops in the tour's history. Londres had hunted down two of the tour's hot favourites, the brothers Henri and Francis Péllssier, and a third rider, drinking hot chocolates at a cafe in Coutances in north-west France. They'd just abandoned the tour, mid-race, following a dispute with the organisers earlier that morning, and they complained to Londres about their treatment and how they had suffered terribly from start to finish.

The race was so gruelling, they said, they needed help to get through the race. They then produced a bag with cocaine for their eyes, chloroform for their gums, and boxes full of pills. 'When we ride,' they said, 'we ride on dynamite'.

* * *

In 1959, eight Kansas City high-school football players were blamed in *Time* magazine for igniting a new wave of abuse of amphetamines in Missouri. Two years earlier, they'd travelled to Oklahoma City for a football game and were introduced to the Valo inhaler, manufactured by Pfeiffer Company in St Louis. Intended for simply clearing a stuffy nose, the inhaler sold for just 75 cents at local pharmacies but contained 200 milligrams of methamphetamine. On their trip away, the Kansas City football players were shown by Oklahoma locals how to extract the methamphetamine and inject it with a hypodermic needle – and when they returned home they promptly passed on their new set of skills.

A frustrated police narcotics boss said Kansas City quickly had 200 locals who were abusing the Valo inhaler for kicks, and those were just the ones they knew about. He reckoned there were probably twice as many as that. The cops were arresting them at a rate of about ten a week for crimes ranging from burglaries to muggings to theft. The drug didn't discriminate, he said. Meth users were spread from the city's swankiest suburbs to its most downtrodden, with sales of the Valo inhaler running 1000 a week above average.

The police boss recounted one recent arrest where a 22-year-old man had ordered tea at a drugstore, promptly poured the hot water into the Valo inhaler, and then jumped into a photo booth in the store where he took six photos of himself shooting up. When he was arrested he told the cops he was trying to impress his friends and illustrate the correct technique. He received a 60-day sentence.

The arrival of the inhaler was also frustrating as authorities in the United States had only recently breathed their own sigh of relief after the manufacturers of the Benzedrine inhaler finally took amphetamine out of their product. Convicts were being smuggled the amphetamine-soaked paper from inside the Benzedrine inhalers and eating them, then going-on drug-fuelled rampages.

In 1959, Pfeiffer Company promised to remove the meth out of their inhaler, due to the widespread abuse.

* * *

At around the same time as the Kansas City footballers were buying up meth inhalers, back here in Oceania athletes were turning to pep pills for performance.

In 1957, a former Australian Olympic swimmer turned journalist, Judy Joy Davies, wrote an article saying that some, but not all, of Australia's top swimmers were taking Benzedrine and Dexedrine in order to shatter race records. The pills were giving the swimmers 'a bit of zing'. The report was described as nonsense the following day by Australia's head Olympic coach, who promised the public no Australian swimmer had ever taken a stimulating drug.

A year earlier, the Waikato Cycling Association wrote a letter of complaint to the national body alleging that many riders had been taking pep pills at the recent national champs and Olympic qualifiers that had been held in Karapiro. The concerned officials said the more they had delved into the matter, the stronger their suspicions had become.

In 1972, *The New Zealand Herald* reported that all athletes were being put on notice, including New Zealanders. If they were caught taking pep pills at the upcoming Munich Olympics they would face enormous penalties. Stimulant use at the previous two Olympics was said to be so rife, the International Olympic Committee estimated that 60 per cent of cyclists were taking pep pills as were athletes across multiple other codes.

And speed and meth were not just being taken by those with two legs.

Following the prominent cases of race horses given Benzedrine in Australia, in October 1954, Auckland Racing Club officials launched a crackdown. They announced that on the upcoming Saturday race meet, they would randomly select two winning horses by way of ballot to test them for traces of drugs. One slight hurdle to overcome: no racing official had ever swabbed a horse for drugs before. So, in order to train race stewards on the correct procedure, the club brought in a horse, Master Richard, and gave him a jolly good dose of Benzedrine, then sent him out to gallop around the Ellerslie track for an hour. Master Richard was then subjected to a urine test and had his mouth and teeth swabbed for five minutes with diluted acetic acid, the samples put into jars and flown to Wellington where a chemist analysed them for traces of drugs.

In the late 1960s, just across town, at the Auckland Trotting Club in Epsom, the pacer Pocket Edition tested positive for methamphetamine after a urine sample following a race meeting. The horse's part owner, Mr Botica, was banned from the sport for 12 months for failing to prevent the drug being administered to his horse and fined $50, while Pocket Edition was disqualified.

That administering meth to horses was a decades-old practice was clearly not known when 50 years later the *Manawatū Standard* reported in 2014 that for the first time in New Zealand a horse had tested positive for methamphetamine. Local trainer Tracy Newton was disqualified for three years after her horse, I'm Not Ticklish, won at decent odds at a meet in Hawera and promptly tested positive for meth. Newton denied doping her horse, telling officials that lax security at the racecourse's stables must have enabled a rival to drug the horse with meth and set her up, but she didn't appeal her disqualification, deciding instead that she no longer had any desire to be part of the racing industry. The methamphetamine had obviously done wonders for I'm Not Ticklish's speed and endurance because, in its next three meth-free starts, it finished last by 10, 20 and 55 lengths, respectively.

It was also at the Hawera racecourse, in 2005, that champion jockey Lisa Cropp was informed that she had returned a positive sample for methamphetamine at a previous meet, and despite Cropp successfully dragging the case out for years, she was eventually banned from racing for nine months. In *Riding with the Devil, Me and 'P': the Lisa Cropp Story*, journalist and editor Mike Dillon details how the top jockey's mind unravelled due to abuse of methamphetamine, how other jockeys would notice her talking to the walls in the women's jockey room, and horse owners endured her incoherent babbling. Cropp was banned again in 2014, this time for three years, after returning another positive methamphetamine test. It was said Cropp had repeatedly refused urine tests or deliberately spoiled her samples. This time she admitted to investigators that she'd been smoking methamphetamine heavily for years and said at her hearing that she was at rock bottom and off to rehab. 'I believe I have more to offer the industry,' she said. 'I love horses, I love riding, I love what I do.'

In January 2022, horse trainer Rochelle Lockett's mare Be Flexi tested positive for methamphetamine after winning a race at the Ōtaki-Māori Racing Club. Investigators also found traces of meth in the horse float, and while Lockett told investigators she had no idea how Be Flexi had been doped, she admitted smoking meth a few days earlier on her fiftieth birthday.

Nearly 70 years after racing officials deliberately doped Master Richard with amphetamine, the racing integrity board told Lockett there were serious animal welfare issues to consider and that horse racing could lose its social licence, and become unacceptable to the public, as they banned her for three years.

* * *

In a small rural town in Georgia in the southern United States there's a race track on a pecan farm called Rancho El Centenario where horses live their lives a quarter mile at a time. It's the equine version of *The Fast and the Furious*. Mainly Mexican punters, who've paid their $100 entry fee, line the short, straight track and gamble on the horses racing at breakneck speed down the course.

What makes Rancho El Centenario unusual is that it sits outside of the state racing commission and outside of any regulations and oversight. It's part of a bush circuit where doping is not only tolerated but also done brazenly; where horses have syringes full of narcotics plunged into their necks just before they race, while they're on the track and in front of the fans.

Undercover animal rights activists from the group People for the Ethical Treatment of Animals (PETA) spent ten months investigating Rancho El Centenario, covertly filming trainers jabbing their horses with chemical cocktails, later posting all their footage on YouTube, and collecting and sending some of the discarded syringes for testing. The results showed the horses were variously being injected with methamphetamine, cocaine, Ritalin and caffeine. PETA announced the unregulated race track was a free-for-all for drugging; that the horses were regularly whipped and given electric shocks. That injured horses were occasionally shot dead right on the track didn't impress PETA much either. Similar race tracks are known to operate in more than 20 other US states.

* * *

Meth doesn't just boost the performance of humans and horses. In November 2020, a greyhound, Zipping Sarah, won her race at Addington Raceway in Christchurch and picked up $4000 in prize money. But it wasn't paid out as Zipping Sarah tested positive for methamphetamine. Her owner, Angela Turnwald, told investigators she didn't have a clue how her dog had come to be doped, but she was eventually banned from the sport for 18 months.

Thrilling Freddy won $10,000 when he took out a race at the Auckland Greyhound Racing Club in Manukau in mid-2022 and then also tested positive for meth. His trainer, Marie Prangley, said she hadn't deliberately doped him and his positive result must have been from accidental cross-contamination. As she too was banned from the sport, Prangley told racing board officials she'd been using methamphetamine on and off for 16 years but that she even wore gloves when handling the dogs to try to prevent contamination from occurring. She told them that was the last thing she would want to happen as she loved her dogs very much.

Other animals have been deliberately doped. A few years ago, scientists at the government science agency ESR in Wellington sent a Canterbury University student some of their top-quality crystal methamphetamine, between 90 and 100 per cent pure. As part of her master's thesis, Courtney Lowther was trying to figure out if repeated doses of methamphetamine would make young hooded rats more aggressive.

Twice a day over 11 days, Lowther injected the rats and then monitored their behaviour to see if they bit, attacked, boxed or reacted with greater hostility to intruder rats than the rats in the control group not on P. Early on in the experiment, the rats on P were actually significantly less inclined to start a ruckus than the control rats. Towards the end of the 11 days, the P rats and control rats were evenly matched in aggression. It appeared that despite all their meth, they were still just rats in a cage. But when Lowther retested the rats a few weeks later, when they were now deemed adults, she found the rats in the meth group were much quicker to bite an enemy and take up an aggressive stance, leading her to conclude that meth use in adolescence might make you more violent later on.

**

For nearly a century now, armies and athletes alike have turned to these powerful stimulants as they look for any means to boost their performance and endurance and outcompete their rivals whether they be on the battlefield or the sports field. But for many decades amphetamines and methamphetamine were simply a run-of-the-mill part of everyday life in New Zealand, as they were around the world. Ordinary folk didn't think twice about purchasing amphetamines at their pharmacy to help them clear up a pesky cold or swallowing meth pills in order to shed a few unwanted pounds, it was often literally just what the doctor ordered.

Their ability to unleash a big burst of energy didn't go unnoticed either.

CHAPTER 2

AMPHETAMINES: 'A BOON TO MANKIND'

Uses and Misuses, Politicians and Committees

IT WAS AN EARLY START AT THE AKERS' FAMILY WOOLSHED IN Ōpiki, Horowhenua, in early January 1955, as it once again played host to a world-record attempt at shearing the most sheep in a nine-hour day.

Step right up, Charlie Oliver. The big, strong 35-year-old shearer from Te Kūiti was into his first sheep at 5 am that morning as part of his shot at the record — which he'd been quietly organising for weeks. Few in the shearing community even knew it was going down until just a day or two beforehand.

By contrast, two years earlier, Te Puke shearer Godfrey Bowen had set a new world record, 456 sheep over nine hours, in front of an estimated 2000 spectators who had packed into and around the same woolshed to watch, some even climbing into the rafters to gain a vantage point and watch history being made. Bowen smashed the old record of 409 sheep, set 12 years earlier in Taranaki, but Bowen's record didn't stand for long; his brother Ivan beat his record by just one sheep the following year.

Now it was Charlie Oliver's turn to have a crack of his own.

And he got off to a flyer, shearing 53 sheep in his first hour, 54 the next, and as shearing expert and author Des Williams reported many years later for the Golden Shears competition programme, some watching that day just didn't believe Charlie Oliver would be able to keep up the pace.

What they didn't know was that he had helpers. His attempt was fuelled by amphetamines – or speed as it's also known – and the Benzedrine pills he kept popping were not only completely legal back then, they were widely available and commonly used. As the morning progressed, Oliver remained well on track and by lunchtime he was sitting seven sheep ahead of the current record.

But at about 1.15 that afternoon, he began looking distressed and disorientated, eventually staggering from the woolshed and not returning. He later collapsed and died that evening in Palmerston North Hospital. The Coroner's inquest into the death found that he had been taking the pills to 'boost his strength' and it warned that they should only be taken under medical supervision, while the pathologist warned that the pills acted as a powerful stimulant, which could be dangerous in certain circumstances. The cause of death was said to be dehydration and overheating due to the enormous physical exertion in hot weather.

Commenting on the incident in April that year, Sydney University's professor of pharmacology, Roland Thorp, said that fatigue and exhaustion are nature's danger signals when someone is physically exerting themselves and that pep pills like Benzedrine could encourage people to go far beyond their limits of physical endurance, 'even to the point of death'.

AMPHETAMINES: 'A BOON TO MANKIND'

* * *

Throughout the 1940s and '50s, newspapers up and down the country ran countless advertisements highlighting the benefits of Benzedrine when it came to relieving cold and flu symptoms, such as this from *Otago Daily Times*, July 1950:

> Benzedrine inhaler: in addition to its pleasant odour it contains a medical ingredient, Amphetamine ... its cool, refreshing vapour reaches areas often inaccessible to fluids, opens congested airways and brings prompt, welcome relief.

Available in every chemist, the Benzedrine inhalers could be carried conveniently in pockets or handbags and could be used discreetly at any time, marketers assured the public, just two snorts up each nostril and 'prolonged relief is yours instantly'. And Benzedrine wasn't just good at combatting hay fever and colds. In 1937, newspapers carried stories from the English scientific journal *The Lancet* showing how experiments at a psychiatric hospital in the United Kingdom had indicated Benzedrine could be a cure for shyness.

Patients who were given the amphetamine became noticeably more talkative, there was a lift in their moods, with some regaining full self-confidence, others talked for the first time since their admission. Doctors also tested the patients' mental abilities and found they were much better at addition and sums after taking the drug than they were before. One patient who had struggled badly with concentration even picked up a newspaper and read it before the stunned doctor's eyes.

The *Te Awamutu Courier* carried a column in 1938 from a New South Wales correspondent who wrote that the latest research in Australia showed that Benzedrine was not addictive or 'a dope' like cocaine or heroin, and was by and large relatively harmless. Its effect was much like a large dose of black coffee, they reported, the user gets the same wakeful boost of spirits and confidence, although they did note some 'over-susceptibles' could experience insomnia, loss of appetite and palpitations.

The *Hokitika Guardian* meanwhile reported Benzedrine was becoming known as the 'killer of fatigue' and included the tale of a recent squash match in which a former British champion who took two tablets before going on court proceeded to play a lightning-fast game. The champ walked from the court, breathing easily, telling observers that the squash ball had appeared as big as a football, while his reactions and ability to think quickly were vastly enhanced.

* * *

In 1939, though, amphetamine's potential for abuse was highlighted. The novelist, poet, journalist and unofficial Press Gallery reporter Iris Wilkinson, who wrote under various noms de plume including Robin Hyde, was found dead in her London apartment.

Her family had set sail for New Zealand shortly after Iris was born in Cape Town in 1906, and settled in the suburb of

Northland in Wellington. At just 17, Iris began working for the *Dominion* newspaper and soon gained her own column, Parliamentary Peeps, in which she covered Parliament's sittings from the Ladies' Gallery. She became close friends with numerous politicians. Throughout her short career, she worked for multiple publications around the country, along the way scandalising several small towns with her high-octane and rather public love affairs. But it was a knee injury in her late teens and a prescription for morphine to help deal with the post-surgery pain that led to a lifelong on-again off-again habit of abusing opiates like heroin.

New Zealand historian and writer Redmer Yska wrote that after the death of her newborn son, Wilkinson was getting wasted day in and day out. Or, as she herself said: 'I began to drug in so indiscriminate a way that you'd have laughed at it. I didn't know the names of anything, every night I thought "I won't wake up tomorrow".'

As a journalist at *The Observer* in Auckland in the early 1930s, Wilkinson covered the rise in the number of overdoses and murders that were being attributed to the barbiturate Veronal, and commented on why people were choosing to abuse drugs: 'The crushing wheels of the twentieth century – overstrain, overwork, financial worry, noise, bustle – have brought about the reign of narcotic poisons.'

By the late 1930s, Wilkinson had travelled to London to try and make her fortune. Instead, she wound up depressed and poverty stricken and liberally began using Benzedrine, hailed at the time for its ability to relieve anxiety and clear the mind. With war in Europe about to break, the New Zealand High

Commissioner helped arrange a fare to get her back home, but when he visited her Kensington accommodation he found her dead. Iris Wilkinson had overdosed on Benzedrine on 23 August 1939. She was 33.

But while there were isolated incidents of harm, amphetamines just weren't considered to be that big a deal and the public hardly batted an eye at their use. In 1951, for example, newspapers reported that the colourful and controversial marathon pianist, New Zealander Jim Montecino, who held the world record for the most hours of continuous play, was still playing strongly and still appeared quite fresh after 84 hours straight at the keys, helped by constant cigarette smoking and two Benzedrine tablets.

Yet it was also clear that amphetamines didn't always enhance the user's performance.

In the mid-1950s, a group of Wellington taxi drivers chased and boxed-in a vehicle whose driver had crashed into one of theirs and then promptly driven off. Behind the wheel was a local doctor who had just completed the night shift at Wellington Hospital and who had taken two Benzedrine tablets to help keep him awake. When the doctor appeared in front of a judge, he said he hadn't predicted how the amphetamine would interact with the two whiskies he'd also consumed and he'd found himself highly intoxicated. He was duly fined 50 pounds and lost his licence for a year.

In addition to Benzedrine, methamphetamine tablets were also being sold to the public under the brand name Methedrine. By the early 1960s, reports of Methedrine misadventures began to emerge.

There was the 18-year-old tourist from California, David Miller, who was convicted after getting caught trying to sell 100 Methedrine tablets to locals. 'They will pick you up' he promised a customer in an Auckland coffee lounge, who promptly dobbed him in and got him locked up.

In Wellington in 1965, Civil Aviation warned New Zealand pilots against taking too many pep pills before flying, which it said was not only habit-forming but could make them dangerously over-confident in the cockpit.

Another Wellington doctor was put on probation and ordered to undergo psychiatric evaluation in 1968 after pleading guilty to obtaining Methedrine using false pretences. He'd been travelling around the lower North Island visiting other doctors, where he would use false identities and claim to have epilepsy in order to obtain dozens of Methedrine pills that the court was told he was hooked on.

And 19-year-old fireman David Pope no doubt will have rued the day back in 1970 when he hooked a buddy up with six of his mum's Methedrine tablets. His mate took them all at once and spent most of the next two days awake, his behaviour drawing the attention of the Christchurch Drug Squad. When interviewed, he promptly ratted his source out and Pope soon found himself in custody.

Meanwhile the chemists that sold pep pills were sporadically being rolled for their supplies. In November 1957, 1500 Benzedrine pills were stolen from a chemist on Auckland's Dominion Road, the third time the chemist had been hit since June. In 1967, a chemist in Auckland's Three Kings was burgled and more than 4000 vials, tablets and capsules of Benzedrine,

Dexedrine and Methedrine were stolen. The shop owner told the press he couldn't think of any possible reason at all why anyone would want such a large quantity of drugs, before adding that the thieves would probably try to sell them.

The main manufacturer of Methedrine in New Zealand, Burroughs Wellcome, stopped selling the product, and another stimulant, Dexamphoid, in 1970, over addiction concerns. In a letter to *The Press* the following year, the company's medical adviser, Dr Wilson, wrote that he had followed with interest the publicity concerning the indiscriminate prescribing of the product. He acknowledged Methedrine had enjoyed widespread popularity in New Zealand for the treatment of obesity but announced the company had destroyed all of its remaining stock of the drug, which he said would have been worth $1 million on the black market, or around $17 million worth of meth today. This showed, he said, how Burroughs Wellcome put people before profit. Why the black-market costs were given for completely legal drugs that were destroyed wasn't explained.

Another company with ample supplies of methamphetamine in the country at the time was the drug wholesaler HF Stevens, and in March 1971, thieves broke into their warehouse in Wainoni, Christchurch. After climbing in through a window and breaking several padlocks, they used an oxy-acetylene welder's torch to burn an 18-inch hole in the security room wall and escape with more than $460 worth of drugs, the equivalent of thieving around $8000 of drugs today. Christchurch detectives would not reveal to the media exactly which drugs were taken, but said they would be worth many thousands of dollars on the black market. The report noted that HF Stevens was known to hold substantial quantities of both methamphetamine and opium, which it used in cough medicines.

In 1963, a former casual employee of HF Stevens, 19-year-old Russell Moffitt, who had admitted pilfering chemicals from the company, found himself standing in the dock of the Christchurch Magistrate's Court charged with the murder of 22-year-old Alison Harper, a first-year arts student at Canterbury University.

Harper had accepted an impromptu invitation from Moffitt to go to the pictures on 22 August and had swung by his flat for a coffee on the way there, but not long after finishing the coffee, she began to feel ill and noticed there had been crystals in the bottom of the cup and that it tasted unusually bitter. Harper soon collapsed and was rushed to Christchurch Hospital, where it was found she'd been poisoned. Moffitt admitted he had been mixing chemicals in the coffee cup in his flat earlier that day. When he was sent home to collect the coffee cup he took the opportunity to throw most of the chemicals in his flat into the Avon River.

Alison Harper died the following morning, and when Moffitt was interviewed later that day, multiple Methedrine pills that had been found in Moffitt's wallet and handed over.

'I gathered he had some dozens of them but he was very reluctant to say where he had got them from or to whom he had subsequently given them,' a government analyst told the court during the murder trial. Moffitt admitted he'd been experimenting at home with a range of chemicals known to be aphrodisiacs, including Cantharidin, a toxic chemical excreted by varieties of blister beetles, but denied trying to drug Alison so he could have sex with her. Moffitt was convicted of manslaughter and sentenced to five years in prison.

* * *

With pep pills being used globally at the time, and in large quantities, in the 1940s the US jazz musician Harry 'The Hipster' Gibson wrote a song that was a commentary on the widespread use of Benzedrine. And while 'Who put the Benzedrine in Mrs Murphy's Ovaltine?' was wildly popular, the lyrics – describing Mrs Murphy's dramatic weight loss as a result of the drug – saw The Hipster get blacklisted by radio stations across America.

It wasn't just Benzedrine and Methedrine used for weight loss. Another very available amphetamine product here, Dexedrine, proved so immensely popular that the 'jump in sales' had the health department worried as far back as 1950. Officials began urging New Zealanders to only take it in accordance with medical advice. Minister of Health Jack Watts was questioned in Parliament about the rampant Dexedrine use by the public, but MPs across the House burst into laughter when he was asked if the booming trade in Dexedrine, with its appetite-suppressing attributes, might be connected to a recent surge in food prices.

By the 1970s, politicians were raising concerns about the abuse of pep pills, particularly by students and rally car drivers. In discussing the Narcotics Amendment Bill in August 1970, which toughened penalties for illegal drugs, including doubling the maximum penalty for dope peddlers from 7 to 14 years in prison, the MP for New Lynn, Jonathan Hunt, spoke about the impact legal amphetamines were having on society. He discussed the 'tragic case' of a gifted young student who took Benzedrine so he could study for 72 hours non-stop in the run-up to an important exam. In that exam, however, Hunt told Parliament, the student wrote the same one word over and over again, for three hours straight! While he was doing nothing against the law, he was experimenting with drugs, which was becoming 'a serious social problem' according to Hunt, who voted for tougher new laws – while at the same time predicting it wouldn't have any impact on drug trafficking or offending. The real solution to drug abuse, he said, was through educational and social means.

Fifty years on Hunt's prediction that tougher penalties wouldn't actually deter drug use looks to have stood the test of time and yet that reality hasn't stopped countless politicians from voting for harsher drug punishments, just as he did.

A year before Hunt spoke of the case of the tragic student, the National MP for Rangiora, Herbert Lorrie Pickering, took a different view on stimulants, telling Parliament that as long as they were in the right hands, they could be hugely beneficial: 'We know, too, that amphetamine, correctly used to promote alertness in an emergency, can be a boon to mankind.'

In an earlier parliamentary debate on forcibly detaining alcoholics, the Labour MP for Sydenham, Mabel Howard, listed amphetamines as among the drugs New Zealanders were growing increasingly worried about, noting that pep pills like Methedrine and Benzedrine 'have become almost as easy to buy as aspirin.' Of primary concern for Howard, though, was marijuana and the emerging drug LSD, 'now famous as the drug which gives you a trip to heaven or to hell'.

While the overuse of pep pills was being raised in Parliament, domestic drug abuse wasn't really on the public's radar to any great extent until the late 1960s.

In the 1930s it was estimated that the number of drug abusers in New Zealand did not exceed 40 or 50 individuals, and nearly all enforcement to date had been focused on catching and punishing Chinese people who were consuming opium. It was as early as 1901 that the Opium Prohibition Act gave police the right to carry out warrantless searches of Chinese people's homes and businesses if they suspected opium was being consumed on site. Another law passed a few years later banned the selling of opium products, but again, only to Chinese people.

Then in 1968, a committee consisting of public health officials, pharmacists, an anthropologist, educators, a senior police representative and chaired by Deputy-Director of Health Geoffrey Blake-Palmer was set up to investigate the levels of drug abuse here. They spent a year travelling the country to hear submissions and gather information and in early 1970 it published its first report, Drug Dependency and Drug Abuse in New Zealand, which found that while improper use of drugs had a long history in New Zealand, it affected such a small segment of the population, it had not been regarded as a threat to the health and wellbeing of the country. But recently, they noted, Aotearoa had drawn international attention and condemnation, along with Finland and Italy, as having the highest per capita use in the world for heroin, because so much of it was being prescribed, with around 50 people becoming hooked. They also noted that the prescribing of barbiturates, which are powerful sedatives used to treat insomnia and anxiety, had jumped 35-fold between 1941 and 1955.

From 1955 to 1963, fewer than 40 people a year were charged with drug offences, and these were usually Chinese people caught with opium. But by the time of the report in 1970, much had changed and the number of non-Chinese people being charged with drug offences had soared (153 offenders) due to a spate of robberies. In 1968, 118 pharmacies were burgled, along with 37 doctors' surgeries and seven wholesalers, a whopping ten-fold increase from the year before.

The committee was concerned New Zealand was following in the footsteps of countries like the UK, Sweden and Japan, which had all recently experienced huge spikes in amphetamine use, and there was a growing trend among young people to crush and inject amphetamines.

The New Zealand Government was concerned at the trends abroad and made a series of moves to restrict access to meth and amphetamines.

They noted that amphetamine use in New Zealand was common among 'obese middle-aged women' and that pep pills were effective as appetite suppressants for a limited time, but there was increasing evidence from doctors and pharmacies that they were rather ineffective in achieving weight loss but quite excellent at producing dependency – 'patients may become nervous, jittery, even frankly psychotic'. Some doctors working at university health services were now refusing to prescribe amphetamines at all because they were so highly sought after by students in the run-up to exams. The committee said amphetamines were now rightly starting to be regarded as dangerous drugs, particularly methamphetamine, which when injected could provide euphoria so intense it was 'often compared to that of sexual orgasm'.

In its recommendations to the government, the committee urged the Department of Health to restrict doctors' ability to issue verbal or telephoned prescriptions for amphetamines to cases of emergency only, and warned doctors to be on the lookout for people seeking large amounts of amphetamines. They called for amphetamines to be more securely stored at pharmacies and warehouses and advocated for the Poisons Act to be amended to make the possession of needles and syringes an offence, due to the growing trend of crushing tablets and injecting amphetamines.

Three years later, in a follow-up investigation into drug abuse and dependency, it was estimated that 4800 New Zealanders were taking pep pills legally on any given day, and nearly a fifth of those were taking methamphetamine. The pep pills were available through the subsidised pharmaceutical programme known as the Drug Tariff, and were said to be very cheap to buy. Not only were thousands of Kiwi adults taking prescribed meth and speed, the Drug Tariff system meant taxpayers were covering 12 per cent of the cost of methamphetamine prescriptions; it was publicly subsidised P.

As global and domestic concerns grew regarding the potential for abuse of amphetamine and methamphetamine pep pills, officials and government ministers further restricted their supply and use to hospitals only. And in 1975, amphetamine and methamphetamine became Class-B controlled drugs under the Misuse of Drugs Act, bringing stiff penalties for their supply and possession. Methamphetamine was no longer widely available, and for the next decade or two it kept a relatively low profile.

When it re-emerged, much had changed. The drug was not being produced by pharmaceutical companies anymore or consumed in standard doses, and doctors and chemists had no oversight of the supply. While it had been used legally here for decades, methamphetamine was about to undergo an image makeover. It was about to gain a reputation for being the most dangerous and destructive drug in the world.

Meth was going underground, and violence often surrounded it.

CHAPTER 3

'SPAWN OF THE DEVIL'
New Zealand Gets Mad on Meth

SUSAN COUCH HAD ARRIVED BRIGHT AND EARLY FOR WORK at the RSA in Auckland's Panmure on Saturday morning, 8 December 2001. Her part-time role as a clerk on weekends to count the bar takings and pokies from the night before suited her to a T, allowing the solo mum to arrange childcare for her kids. Just weeks out from Christmas, the end-of-year work functions and festivities were in full swing as the city wound down for the summer.

By 7 am, Susan's colleagues were also there – club president Bill Absolum, cleaner Mary Hobson and club member Wayne Johnson – all helping set up for the day ahead. About half an hour later, Susan was interrupted by what appeared to be a policeman knocking at the door and she opened it to see what was up. But the man wearing the police shirt was no officer of the law but a 23-year-old violent criminal, William (Willie) Bell, who had worked briefly as a barman at the RSA four months earlier, before being fired. Susan later recalled that 'the penny dropped' almost as soon as she opened the door, but by then Bell had produced a shotgun, and after beating Susan to within an inch of her life, spent the next 45 minutes using the butt of the shotgun to bludgeon to death Bill Absolum and Mary Hobson.

He also shot and killed Wayne Johnson and made off with $13,000 in cash and cigarettes – although the money didn't last long. It was quickly spent on a new sound system and tinted windows for both his and his accomplice's cars.

The night before the attack, Bell had been drinking at the Manukau rugby league club and smoking meth outside a Māori Wardens' Christmas function before more drinking with mates, including his planned get-away driver, Darnell Tupe. But Bell took so long inside the RSA killing the staff that morning that Tupe actually fled and drove home. During the trial his partner told the court he had started crying when he later saw the killings on TV.

Bell said he'd blacked out on meth during his frenzied attack, his family members saying he'd been using heavily ever since he left prison a few months earlier. 'He was so hooked on the shit,' as his brother put it, 'his eyes were always expanded.' In court, Bell admitted he was smoking several hits of P a day in the weeks leading up to the killing, and that he was out on parole at the time, only released from Paremoremo Prison a few months earlier where he'd been serving a five-and-a-half-year sentence for a similar crime: he'd nearly bashed a Mangere petrol station worker to death with a stolen police baton, in 1997. He'd been rejected for a job by the gas station's manager earlier that day after turning up for the interview reeking of marijuana; he'd returned that night seeking revenge.

In February 2003, Bell was sentenced to 33 years in prison with no hope of parole, his complete lack of remorse a major factor. It was the longest non-parole sentence ever handed down at the time by five years, although it was reduced by three years on appeal. Susan Couch described it as a hollow victory, saying the damage Bell caused could never be undone. Wayne Johnson's brother told reporters outside the court that Bell should have just been shot and his body dumped at the tip.

* * *

But it was an 11-hour meth-fuelled rampage that occurred just one month before Bell's sentencing that helped cement methamphetamine's reputation in the public's mind as a drug linked to insane violence and unthinkable crime, its users capable of almost unfathomable cruelty, whose minds could become wracked by barely believable psychosis.

A one-man crime wave, running on vast quantities of methamphetamine and variously armed with a samurai sword, a hammer and a homemade submachine gun, Antoine 'Tony' Dixon, placed P firmly in the spotlight.

Like Bell, Dixon was another long-time offender who had committed gross acts of violence well before he ever tried P. On the morning of 21 January 2003, Dixon's new girlfriend, Renee Gunbie, was cleaning their home in the small Hauraki township of Pipiroa. To help complete the chores, she was sipping a cocktail of orange juice mixed with methamphetamine and cocaine. At some point, Dixon entered the house and skolled the cocktail. She later told Dixon's lawyer she couldn't quite figure out how he was still standing and that she was in half a mind to call a doctor. But no sooner did she have that thought than Dixon's eyes turned black and the violence began. He picked up a hammer and broke her arm and smashed her in the head.

Dixon's long-suffering and longer-term girlfriend, Simonne Butler, arrived at the house that evening sometime between 6 and 7 pm to find Gunbie lying under blankets with blood trickling down her forehead – then Dixon turned on her, too, screaming at them both, accusing them of sleeping with police, of being informants, and accusing Butler of using parabolic microphones to record their conversations. Next, he grabbed an ornamental samurai sword that was kept in the house and the chopping began.

Again and again Dixon swung the sword at them. He ordered Butler to bow down and kneel in front of him so that when he chopped off her head it would land in the washing basket because he didn't want a mess. She credits her friend Roger, who she'd picked up and brought to the house with her that evening, with saving their lives by convincing Dixon to end the attack – well, that and the sword breaking on Gunbie's head.

Both women suffered catastrophic injuries as they tried to defend their heads and faces from the sword. They were eventually flown by helicopter from Pipiroa to Auckland for live-saving treatment. Renee Gunbie lost her right hand, but surgeons successfully reattached both of Simonne Butler's, in a marathon 27-hour surgery.

After calling an ambulance saying someone had fallen from the roof of a shed, Dixon jumped in a car with Roger and drove to Hamilton at speeds of up to 160 kilometres per hour, Roger taking turns steering from the passenger seat as Dixon smoked P from a pipe. He then made his way to Auckland – stopping to threaten numerous people at various petrol stations with a firearm before arriving at Highland Park Caltex petrol station. There, 25-year-old James Te Aute and his mates Jackson Lemalu and Craig Grace, who had been smoking methamphetamine themselves, watched as Dixon turned up and began pulling the finger at them and mouthing obscenities.

As Te Aute and Lemalu went to confront him, Dixon grabbed his submachine gun and, from the front seat of his car, unleashed a volley of shots, hitting Te Aute ten times in the back, killing him instantly. He then drove off and picked up a hitchhiker, Bradley Kukard, asking him if he'd heard about the shooting or samurai sword attacks and showing him his gun before telling Kukard he was 'okay' and dropping him off near where he lived.

After firing shots at pursuing police, Dixon burst into a home in Flat Bush and took the owner, Ian Miller, hostage, while his partner managed to escape. Over the course of the next several hours, Dixon informed Miller he'd been spied on recently by a 747 Jumbo Jet that was following him, and that one of the women he attacked had a homing device on her. When he eventually let Miller leave the house and Dixon surrendered to the police at 6 am the next day, he promptly confessed that he had 'cut the bitches up'.

At his trial it was Dixon's sea-anemone-like haircut and his wild eyes the size of small moons that captivated the media, but it was also where the public got an insight into why he'd ended up the way he was. His sister, Carla Dixon-Foxley, flew from the UK to give evidence at the trial, where she described how their mother had subjected him to years of emotional and physical abuse. A devout Jehovah's Witness member, their mother used to call her son 'the spawn of the devil'; she used to chain him to the clothesline in the backyard like a dog and she'd get men from the church to come around and beat him, it was reported. Their Grey Lynn home had been a boarding house and many of the tenants recently released from local psychiatric hospitals. Dixon-Foxley told the court it was like living in a madhouse. Dixon also used to tell people that his mother would lock him in the rooms with the male tenants as punishment and they would sexually abuse him. Sent to a youth facility as a boy, Dixon then spent the rest of his life in and out of prisons.

His lawyer, Barry Hart, argued at his trial that Dixon was clearly insane at the time of the crimes and, given his mental state, to treat him as a 'normal' person just wasn't appropriate. At this, Dixon piped up: 'Bring back the electric chair. Let's do it.' But the jury didn't buy the insanity plea and sentenced him to 20 years without parole. Then, despite his lawyer repeatedly raising concerns about his mental health in the months leading up to early 2009, Dixon was found dead in his cell in Paremoremo Prison on 4 February 2009. After bashing his head against the cell walls and trying to choke himself, Dixon eventually managed to cover a security camera with toilet paper, tie a ligature around his neck and take his own life.

'It was the nicest thing he'd ever done for me,' Simonne Butler wrote in her 2016 autobiography *Double-Edged Sword*. 'His death was a gift'; the universe had answered her prayers. Toxicology reports found traces of meth in his blood and his urine following his death, but Butler said she could have told you that. 'Tony [Dixon] was fried the whole time.' She said that while he was notoriously paranoid, it had got much worse in the weeks preceding the attack. He believed Cessnas, 747s and even satellites were surveilling him, he would phone the police up to 50 times a day urging them to stop following him and he would sit at the kitchen table with a pocket knife trying to dig imaginary electronic tracking devices out of his arms and chest.

Butler claims Dixon had always been paranoid, violent and abusive, and while P may have accelerated his transition to certified psycho-killer, this was inevitable, drugs or no drugs. 'He didn't need P to beat me into unconsciousness or to hurt any of the people in his life. He didn't need P to be paranoid, but it sure made things a lot worse.'

* * *

Because of grisly high-profile crimes like these playing out on the news, P was rapidly establishing itself as public enemy number one and it spurred the government into a series of crackdowns. Firstly, methamphetamine was reclassified from a Class-B to a Class-A drug under the Misuse of Drugs Act. The associate Health Minister in May 2003, Jim Anderton, said he was putting the importers, manufacturers and suppliers of methamphetamine on notice that they were now risking life imprisonment. P was causing havoc in our families and communities, and the move would give the police extra powers, while a Methamphetamine Action Plan he'd announced a week earlier would help reduce supply.

But it appears the P cooks and dealers didn't see that press release because, just a few years later, *The New Zealand Herald* was claiming Aotearoa now had the highest 'P infestation rate' in the world – even though by then meth use here was falling considerably. In 2009, the newspaper urged lawmakers to step up and do more to combat the 'terrible concoction' which it said was causing so much harm to our social fabric and that no one was safe from 'the meth menace': 'It might be slipped to your teenage son or daughter, grandson or grand-daughter, a trusted employee or a business partner ... Once addicted they are easily drawn into the grip of the gangs that manufacture and distribute most of it.'

And at the Novotel Hotel in Auckland on 8 October that year, a room full of police and customs officers, community workers, drug counsellors and the press gathered to hear the government's latest plan to wage war on the drug. 'I'm here to speak about P; methamphetamine, crank, ice, crystal, call it what you will,' Prime Minister John Key told the crowd. 'Everyone in this room knows something of its horrors.'

Key warned that P was a seriously addictive and viciously destructive drug and that users were harming not just themselves but their families and other law-abiding citizens. He said that not only was the average P addict stealing (a very specific) $1840 worth of goods a month to fuel their habit, they were selling $5100 worth of drugs a month, often to children and family.

He touched on the RSA killings, the samurai sword attack and a P-induced car chase down Auckland's motorway earlier that year in which an innocent 17-year-old courier driver and new dad, Halatau Naitoko, had been accidentally shot dead by the Armed Offenders Squad who were trying to stop a criminal with a shotgun from carjacking another motorist. While acknowledging methamphetamine was used elsewhere the prime minister said that, 'Sadly, P is a very New Zealand problem and while some say we can't fight it, it's been around too long, the gangs will never give up, there's nothing we can do, I don't accept that and this National-led government won't accept that.'

As we will soon see, methamphetamine is not just very much a New Zealand problem and it never has been, and in fact, the decisions made by the prime minister that day arguably turned out to be a godsend to the gangs in the long run.

Key vowed his government would confront the P problem and delivered this message to the gangs: 'The government is coming after your business and we will use every tool we have to destroy it. We will be ruthless in our pursuit of you and the evil drug you push.'

And with that John Key outlined his plan for taking on P – $22 million in new funding for clinical services, to allow 3000 people hooked on the drug to seek help; 40 customs officers assigned to dedicated drug-taskforce duties, to help disrupt the supply chain of precursors (the chemicals required to cook meth in underground labs) coming in from abroad, mainly China. Also, from now on, more of the money the police seized from criminals would be redirected to help fund anti-P initiatives, and legislation would be tweaked to make it easier for those addicted to the drug to be forced into compulsory treatment.

The prime minister put public sector bosses on notice that they needed to help deliver on the government's plan. This was going to be a major blow to the P cooks, John Key told his audience, and it was a blow he was pleased to be delivering. At the same time Key was realistic: he knew he simply couldn't promise that P would be stamped out for good. Political leaders the world over who had vowed to end drug use often found it a very elusive goal because, as he acknowledged, drug dealers are notoriously adaptable.

By far and away the sharpest prong in the announcement was the reclassification of pseudoephedrine, the common ingredient in cold and flu medicines, as a Class-B2 controlled drug, meaning that from now on it would only be available in very limited circumstances. But pseudoephedrine was gold to methamphetamine cooks; it was just about all they needed to get started. For years, meth cooks had been employing people, known as 'smurfers' overseas, to buy up as much pseudoephedrine as they could. In the mid-2000s, it was estimated a smurf could buy $100 worth of Sudafed or Coldrex or Coldral and be paid $300 for it by a cook. Once extracted, that pseudoephedrine could make several thousand dollars' worth of methamphetamine. And with returns like that, less-subtle methods of acquiring it became popular too, like driving stolen vehicles at high speeds through pharmacy front doors late at night to steal all their supplies of cold and flu medicine.

At his wits end after being burgled three times in three weeks in 2003, Matamata chemist Peter McSweeney spent $20,000 turning his two chemist shops into fortresses, with bollards, iron gates and 24/7 security cameras in a bid to stop the repeat ram-raids and smash-and-grabs. Castlecliff Pharmacy in Whanganui was the scene of a ram-raid in January 2007 when thieves drove a vehicle into their business at 3.15 am and took two shelves worth of pseudoephedrine cold and flu medicine; the pharmacist telling the local paper the robbers knew exactly what they were after and that it wasn't the first time her shop had been targeted. In Auckland the same year, police asked for the public's help in identifying a 'low-key' man they believed had robbed eight pharmacies across the city. Officers said his MO was always the same: he'd casually walk into a chemist shortly before lunch or closing time and demand their pseudoephedrine products while implying he was armed. In the latest robbery, the staff in a pharmacy on Dominion Road said they thought he'd shown them a stun gun.

Not long after, a career crook in the South Island with a penchant for ram-raiding and robbing pharmacies gained notoriety after repeatedly outrunning and outfoxing police for half a year. William (Billy) Stewart's time on the run and skirmishes with the law spawned a run of t-shirts, a folk song and even made a few headlines around the world. There were suggestions he was New Zealand's own Ned Kelly. His game of cat and mouse with police began shortly after Stewart, a heavy cannabis and frequent meth user in his mid-40s, was released from prison in 2008 after bashing and threatening to kill his girlfriend in a Nelson motel three years earlier. Nabbed while out on parole for possessing cannabis, Stewart failed to appear in court, sparking a warrant for his arrest. When next spotted by police, he promptly outran them and began one of New Zealand's longest manhunts.

One reporter described him as 'An outlaw who lived off his wits in the South Island bush, escaped police in high-speed chases down Canterbury's dirt roads, offered lifts to hitchhikers, and carved thank-you notes in tables at houses he raided for food and shelter.' But it was an etched note left on the table of a smoko room on a Canterbury farm, 'Thanks guys, Billy the Hunted One', that helped ignite the lore that we had a shaggy-haired folk hero, with the farmer reporting Stewart had helped himself to coffee and a meal of a couple of hot pies.

While on the run, Stewart robbed multiple pharmacies, often hitting several on the same night, frequently using a sledgehammer to break windows and empty the shelves of cold and flu medications. On 26 January 2009, he robbed a pharmacy in Darfield, Canterbury, in the early morning and another in Methven shortly afterwards. In March, he drove a car straight through the security roller door of a chemist in the Christchurch suburb of Halswell and cleared out their stocks of pseudoephedrine, then immediately drove half an hour to Leeston where he rolled another pharmacy.

His popularity infuriated the local police. One senior cop told the media that Billy the Hunted One was nothing more than a scumbag thief and druggie who would rob his own grandmother to get what he wanted. When eventually caught by armed police, Stewart apparently told the arresting officers that he'd had a good run. In court, he was accused of stealing and damaging nearly $400,000 worth of property. His rap sheet included 23 burglaries, five stolen vehicles, three dangerous high-speed car chases, ramming two police cars and being in possession of a pipe to smoke methamphetamine.

It wasn't always necessary to use brute force or threats in order to obtain the valuable precursor from chemists, however.

In fact, during the mid-2000s, the Unichem Pharmacy in Pukekohe went out of its way to cater for those looking to purchase large amounts of pseudoephedrine. The retired pharmacist and sole employee, Samuel Pulman, would open the pharmacy shortly after 6 am, nearly two hours early, and sell large quantities of cold and flu tablets to his early-bird customers. When the police cottoned on to the operation and installed covert cameras, it was revealed that Pulman was selling the medicine at $100 cash per box, three times their normal sale price and to dozens of customers.

Finally arrested, Pulman admitted selling nearly 1300 boxes of cold and flu drugs that he knew were going to be used to make P, but he told the court that as well as being fully aware of the police surveillance cameras in the pharmacy, he was actually selling them under instruction from his local community constable in order to help point the cops in the direction of the local meth cooks — rather than being a crook himself, he was simply helping to take them down. The judge didn't buy the good Samaritan defence and Pulman, the 70-year-old who was known locally as 'uncle' and who organised table tennis practices for Pukekohe kids and sold vegetables to help raise funds for the local youth centre, was sentenced to almost six years in prison.

Unsurprisingly, when the police raided some of his regular customers' homes, they found numerous meth labs. One of those caught told them they could turn a packet of cold medicine into a gram of methamphetamine — then worth about $1000 — in about 60 minutes. The number of labs found and dismantled by the cops from 2000–2009 shows the industry escalated at incredible rates, according to New Zealand police data, reducing in the later years.

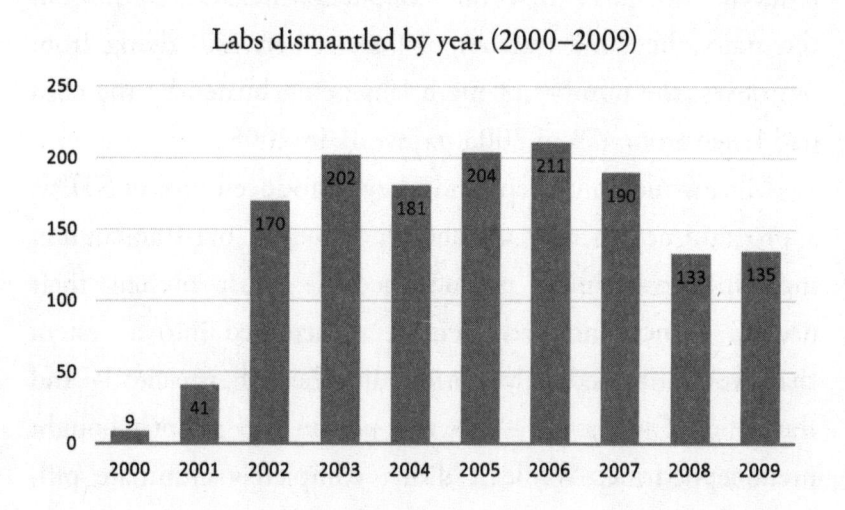

Labs dismantled by year (2000–2009)

Year	Labs
2000	9
2001	41
2002	170
2003	202
2004	181
2005	204
2006	211
2007	190
2008	133
2009	135

A balancing act for the government was that, in removing this ingredient for P cooks, it restricted availability to a substance providing relief for law-abiding citizens when they were feeling under the weather. John Key commissioned his chief science advisor, Sir Peter Gluckman, to investigate the matter. Key said he'd been advised that a safe and effective alternate chemical, phenylephrine, was already used in many cold and flu medications and for most people it was just as effective as pseudoephedrine.

More than a decade on and many New Zealanders dispute Gluckman's advice and frequently bemoan the fact they can't get good-quality medicine packed with pseudoephedrine when they're ill like they could in the good old days; the phenylephrine alternatives just don't cut it. We were following in the footsteps of places like Oregon in the United States which had cracked down on pseudoephedrine sales and then made them prescription only in 2006. While the move hadn't reduced the harm that methamphetamine was causing in the state, the same number of people were still dying from overdoses, the number of meth labs being busted by the cops had fallen from 473 in 2003 to just 21 in 2008.

Meanwhile, in Queensland, they introduced Project STOP, a programme whereby anyone who bought over-the-counter medicines containing pseudoephedrine must present their driver's licence and had their details entered into a system that would immediately notify all other pharmacies – and the police if necessary – that this person had recently bought pseudoephedrine. While it didn't completely eliminate pill-shopping for pseudoephedrine, it clearly acted as a deterrent and resulted in a 39 per cent decrease in the number of meth labs being found around Queensland.

Weighing up the likely downstream effects of eliminating pseudoephedrine domestically, Gluckman noted it could well shift the dial towards more illegal imports of pseudoephedrine from China, manufactured legally there in pill form and known as ContacNT. And Gluckman also quite correctly prophesied that the ban on pseudoephedrine may result in methamphetamine simply being trafficked here from abroad, but noted that reducing the number of clandestine labs would in itself be of value in terms of public health and safety.

And it didn't take long for the ban on the sale of pseudoephedrine to have a big impact on the domestic manufacturing of methamphetamine. The number of clan meth labs detected and dismantled by law enforcement plummeted in the years following the restrictions, to half or even a third of what they had been previously.

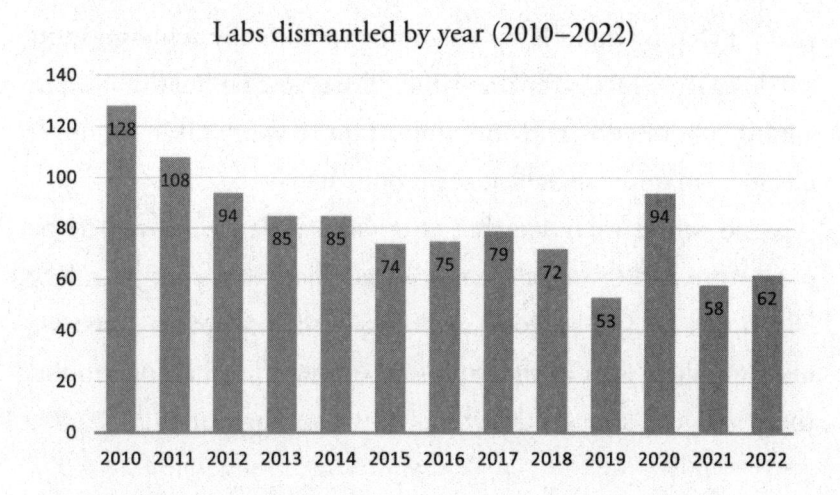

Labs dismantled by year (2010–2022)

Year	Labs
2010	128
2011	108
2012	94
2013	85
2014	85
2015	74
2016	75
2017	79
2018	72
2019	53
2020	94
2021	58
2022	62

John Key declared war on P and the gangs that help manufacture and distribute it in 2009. Three years later, it looked as if the authorities were winning the battle. Along with the reduction in the number of domestic meth labs, a drug-use survey showed the number of New Zealanders who had tried methamphetamine in the past year at 1 per cent – half what it had been a few years previously.

The Drug Foundation's executive director Ross Bell said the fall in the number of P users was enormously significant and that Police and Customs deserved a huge amount of credit for their work as did the government for significantly boosting addiction-treatment funding by $30 million dollars. It was now $120 million a year. And a senior police officer said that society's view on the drug had changed, meaning it was no longer socially acceptable: 'I think we're actually winning, fingers crossed.'

The New Zealand Herald celebrated in 2012 by publishing an editorial, 'Fight against scourge of P almost won', in which it said that it's not often a country can defeat a criminal drug and yet that is what New Zealand has practically achieved in its battle against methamphetamine. 'P has lost its hold on all but a hard core of addicts. More important, few are taking it up. It has lost whatever social cachet it once had.'

And while we'll see that this victory dance proved to be premature and those in the meth trade here did what John Key had noted they're so good at doing – they adapted – first we need to take a look at the explosion in meth production around the world and see exactly who is now cooking our P.

CHAPTER 4

HUNGRY FOR BUSINESS
Overseas Meth Labs and Drug Routes into New Zealand

TRAVELLING IN THREE TRUCKS THROUGH THE BAKWA district, elders had arrived in Farah, a city in Afghanistan, in November 2008, to pick up some donated supplies for their farmers. The governor of Farah Province had announced a short time earlier that he would be distributing 50 tonnes of wheat seed and 50 tonnes of fertiliser to Bakwa farmers, but on one condition: the elders were only to disperse them to those farmers who promised to refrain from the age-old practice of growing poppies that season for the opium trade.

Sitting in the south-west of Afghanistan on the border with Iran, Farah is one of the most sparsely populated provinces in the country, made up of various tribal groups, with nearly three-quarters of its residents farmers, the rest working in sectors supporting those farmers. Governor Amin said the delivery of the wheat seeds was somewhat of a celebration of the improving security situation, while the regional commander of the United Nations International Security Assistance Force, Captain Antonio Bernardo, said the project would help improve both governance and security in the district.

To pay them their dues, many Bakwa farmers did indeed find an alternative to growing poppies but unfortunately for the security forces it wasn't the wholesome wholegrain one they had envisaged.

Over a decade later, on 5 May 2019, United States' war planes carried out attacks across Bakwa and the neighbouring Delaram district on more than 60 sites believed to be clandestine methamphetamine laboratories connected to the Taliban. According to United States' intelligence reports, the methamphetamine was being sold to help fund the Taliban's elite commando Red Units, whose modus operandi was carrying out deadly surprise attacks on motorbike. Revered as highly skilled night fighters, the Red Units were responsible for many lethal strikes on foreign coalition soldiers and they inflicted huge casualties on Afghan National Army troops too. Not only were the bombed meth labs helping fund the Red Units but also those involved in cooking the meth were Taliban fighters, according to American intelligence.

However, the United Nations Humans Rights Office strongly disagreed. It found there were at least 39 civilian casualties in the bombings and it was unable to substantiate dozens more deaths. It said it was clear that women and children who had nothing whatsoever to do with the meth labs had been killed in the attacks. While it acknowledged that the Taliban uses drug-making facilities to fund its operations, the meth labs the US had bombed were not run exclusively by the Taliban but by criminal groups linked to international drug-trafficking networks. Blowing up drug labs wasn't a new practice, although the Human Rights Office said it was the first time there had been so many civilian casualties. The United States disagreed, arguing the meth labs were legitimate military targets and in their eyes, not one civilian had died.

Yet, while more than 60 suspected meth labs were literally blown off the face of the earth that day in Bakwa and Delaram, it didn't appear to put much of a dent in Afghanistan's newfound ability to produce vast amounts of methamphetamine, according to another arm of the United Nations, the Office on Drugs and Crime, which says the country is now a major producer of meth. It found that even after the assault, the amount of meth confiscated in Afghanistan in 2019 was seven times higher than it was just the year before, that a high proportion of young Afghans were now using the drug, and its neighbour Iran was being flooded with Afghan meth.

And the reason Afghanistan started producing so much meth is because they recently realised an essential ingredient was literally growing right in their backyard. The plant ephedra, which grows wild in the mountains of central Afghanistan and which can be harvested by hand, comes in handy if you're looking to make methamphetamine, because it's relatively easy to extract ephedrine from the plant. Known locally as bandar or oman, Afghans have traditionally used ephedra for firewood or in herbal remedies for things like kidney ailments, but now an entire industry has sprung up in Bakwa to turn ephedra into meth. Or that's certainly what the socio-economist Dr David Mansfield and his team found when they investigated the matter for the European Monitoring Centre for Drugs and Drug Addiction (EMCDDA), publishing their report in late 2020.

They found that hundreds of enterprising Bakwa locals have realised there's good money to be made in methamphetamine and that many are now enthusiastically using their homes to make either ephedrine or meth. And the relevance of this for us? Afghan meth is increasingly on New Zealand's radar.

Another drug intelligence report, this one by New Zealand Customs in 2021, noted a dramatic increase in methamphetamine production from the regions of Afghanistan, and that its meth was being trafficked across much of the planet through various routes, and some of it destined for Australian and New Zealand shores.

Back in 2016, Afghan traders had begun buying vast quantities of ephedra from locals in the mountainous provinces and, after drying it for 25 days, would ship it to a bazaar in Bakwa, and from there locals would buy it and begin extracting the ephedrine. After being ground and sieved, the ephedra is mixed with water, petrol, salt and caustic soda and left to soak overnight. After this it's heated in a metal container; a pinch of salt, a lick of car battery acid and xylene are added to the mix and once heated again, the liquid evaporates, leaving a substance that appears like dried yoghurt. Locals told Mansfield's team that extracting ephedrine was so easy anyone could do it and that, in the space of just three years, the number of ephedrine cooks in their town alone had increased from one to thirty.

A 20-kilogram haul of ephedrine can be processed into around 15 kilos of high-quality methamphetamine, but the skills required to cook that meth require much greater smarts and knowledge of chemistry or, as one Bakwa meth cook told the researchers, 'it's technical, it takes time to learn'. Specialist cooks were paid NZ$20 per kilo for meth they produced, double the rate for those making ephedrine.

A kilo of export-quality methamphetamine being produced in Bakwa was being sold for around NZ$440 a kilo in 2020, but the reported profit margins were slim, with producers clearing a little over NZ$30 a kilo. To put that in perspective, depending on how well connected someone is in Aotearoa, a kilo here can cost around $150,000.

In calculating the costs, the EMCDDA report factored in a $25 per kilogram tax that has to be paid to the Taliban, a reality of doing business in that part of the country, lending weight to the UN's argument that while meth may help fund the Taliban's military operations, many of those killed in the US bombings of the province's meth labs in 2019 were not directly connected to the organisation. And fascinatingly, for those in Bakwa who are involved in the extraction of ephedrine or the cooking of meth, there is a one-stop shop where they can buy absolutely everything required to get the job done – the Abdul Wadood Bazaar.

The market has ballooned in recent years and an estimated 2400 truckloads of ephedra are delivered there each year, with an Afghan Security forces raid on the bazaar in 2019, in which some of the stalls were blown up, only a temporary setback. The researchers found it has only continued to expand in size since. The report estimated around 2300 Bakwa locals were employed in ephedrine extraction – from labourers and traders to drivers, guards and the cooks themselves – while around another 200 locals were employed turning that ephedrine into meth. Theoretically, Bakwa was producing enough ephedrine to make 65 tonnes of crystal meth a month.

If all the ephedrine being extracted was being cooked into meth locally (the report estimating you'd need about 500 meth labs to achieve this), the industry in Bakwa would be worth up to NZ$380 million a year and bringing in between NZ$6–7 million in taxes for the Taliban or whichever armed groups were taxing the industry.

Almost 90 per cent of the meth seized in Iran in 2019 was found to be of Afghan origin, showing the Bakwa meth industry is wasting no time capturing a large part of the region's meth market. Figures like those support one of EMCDDA's main observations: Afghanistan's burgeoning meth industry could soon rival its opium economy.

The New Zealand Customs report in 2021 outlined three traditional opium trafficking routes from Afghanistan, mainly by Pakistani nationals, now also used to smuggle meth:

1. the Balkan route: into Iran, Türkay, the Balkan countries, and through to Western and Central Europe
2. the now seldom-used northern route: through central Asia and then through to Europe and Russia
3. the southern route: via Pakistan or Iran to India and then to Africa, particularly South Africa, Kenya, Ethiopia, Mozambique, Tanzania, Rwanda, Burundi, Uganda and Madagascar – and shipped to Australasia.

While Customs intercepted a modest 15 kilos of meth from South Africa in 2019 and 25 kilos the following year, along with a couple more kilos from Zimbabwe and Kenya, the report discussed how its counterparts along the southern route were now making marine interceptions of hundreds of kilos of Afghan meth aboard vessels often destined for Australia.

With the very high prices methamphetamine can fetch in Aotearoa, comparatively, Customs warned we were an attractive destination too, and it seems Afghan exporters agree – German authorities intercepted a small 10-kilo shipment of Afghan meth that was on its way here a couple of years back.

But Afghanistan's Bakwa is not alone in being a hotbed for meth production, and Chinese police found that out the hard way when they tried to carry out a raid on locals in the Boshe Village in Lufeng City, Guangdong Province in Southern China in 2013. As security services attempted to enter the village, which despite being only half-a-square kilometre in size, was then home to about 14,000 residents spread among several thousand unnumbered homes, the villagers had clearly been tipped off about the pending raid and offered up furious resistance.

The locals formed roadblocks and when the police tried to move in, they were surrounded by hundreds of villagers on motorbikes who were screaming and shouting and revving their engines. Nail-boards were laid across the roads, and the locals were armed with an arsenal of weapons, including imitation firearms, homemade grenades and crossbows, the good folk of Boshe suggesting it might be a wise idea for their unwelcome guests to leave as they also hurled rocks and abuse down from the rooftops.

Boshe was nicknamed 'China's number one drug village' and 'the Fortress' by locals. It's a village where narcotics police estimated 20 per cent of those living there were actively involved in producing methamphetamine, largely with ephedra they'd import by the truckload from inner Mongolia. Together, with industrious locals from the wider city of Lufeng, they were producing about a third of all the methamphetamine consumed in China in 2013.

A sign at the entrance to Boshe read: 'By Order of the Village Committee: Dumping of meth-cooking waste strictly forbidden'. The villagers had successfully repelled several raids, but early in the morning of 29 December that year, after jamming phone signals in the town, more than 3000 elite paramilitary police, backed up by helicopters and speedboats, launched a surprise attack – Operation Thunder – arresting over 180 locals and seizing 3 tonnes of methamphetamine, 23 tonnes of precursor chemicals, several hundred kilos of ketamine, and dismantling 77 meth labs for good measure. The head of Guangdong's public security and narcotics department, Qiu Wei, admitted afterwards that many of the police who carried out the raid were petrified that the villagers would start tipping the hydrochloric or sulphuric acid used to cook meth down on them from above as they made their way through the narrow alleys of Boshe.

Stacks of cash and gold bars were found in residents' homes, and among those arrested was the Boshe village branch secretary of the Communist Party, Cai Donjia, who became known in China as 'the godfather of crystal meth'. He was accused of using his senior position to both produce meth himself and provide protection for those cooking it, and at his trial in 2016 he was convicted of manufacturing 180 kilos of crystal meth as well as bribing the police to free meth traffickers, and was sentenced to death. In early January 2019, 55-year-old Cai Dongjia was executed.

Chinese journalists were taken on a tour of Boshe in 2018, a village now covered with banners reading 'Wage a people's war against illegal drugs', and anti-drug posters plastered on just about every wall throughout the town. The local police told reporters they could now enter Boshe without opposition, claiming that the entire village had 'gone straight'. Chinese police carried out regular, sometimes daily, searches of villagers' homes, they maintained eight checkpoints on roads near the village and three checkpoints out at sea to stop precursor chemicals getting in and meth getting out.

The reporters noted, though, they didn't see a single adult male during their 30-minute tour of the village; most had been arrested or had fled, while police were still actively hunting around 100 men from Boshe, the youngest 18, the oldest 80 years old. A BBC article from around this same time suggested Boshe had simply transitioned into producing another synthetic drug: ketamine.

In 2021, China's National Narcotics Control Commission estimated 1.2 million of its 1.4 billion citizens were using methamphetamine, and said that they account for more than half of all of China's drug users. It reported that China's meth problem is exacerbated by the vast quantities of meth pills and crystal methamphetamine produced in the Golden Triangle – an area that includes Myanmar, Laos and northern Thailand

– before making its way into China through Yunnan Province. It reported that 98 per cent of the meth which Chinese law enforcement seized in 2019 could be traced to Myanmar.

* * *

Partly ruled by a murderous military junta, and partly completely lawless, Myanmar is now swamping Asia and the Pacific with very high quality and very affordable crystal methamphetamine. It's a country where crystal meth was recently selling wholesale at the meth factory gate for the reasonable price of around NZ$4000 a kilo.

Two decades ago, as we have seen, small-scale domestic methamphetamine labs, often linked to local gangs, were common throughout Australia, New Zealand, the Philippines and Indonesia, but that's not so much the case anymore: Myanmar is servicing this entire region. Because why cook at home when you can order in?

Over the last ten years, the amount of meth being made in Myanmar has gone ballistic – the purity of its meth has skyrocketed while prices have plummeted; a perfect recipe for booming consumption and addiction. Much of the meth is made in Shan State, an area controlled by local rebel warlords, armed drug gangs and gunrunners – an ideal location if you want to set up a methamphetamine super lab; it's an absolute free-for-all. Its geography comes in handy too. Shan State borders China which gives it easy access to supplies of precursors and it also borders Laos and Thailand, opening up convenient trafficking routes into both local and regional drug markets.

As cooking high-quality meth requires skill and chemists, there are also many smaller operations in Shan State where criminal gangs run pill presses and turn the meth powder they've bought from those labs into the lower-quality methamphetamine pills that are so common across Asia.

It was in Shan State in 2020 that the biggest bust of synthetic drugs in South-east Asia's history occurred. Between February and April, Myanmar police and military carried out raids across the state and seized 200 million meth tablets – the equivalent of 18 tonnes of meth – as well as half a tonne of crystal meth, 300 kilograms of heroin, nearly 4000 litres of methylfentanyl – an opioid 50 times stronger than heroin, so strong just a few milligrams can be lethal – and 35 tonnes of precursor chemicals. Thirty-three arrests were made.

The seizure was described as 'off the charts' by Jeremy Douglas, the regional representative of the United Nations Office on Drugs and Crime for South-east Asia and Pacific. When I spoke to him in 2022 he explained that the scale of synthetic drug production in Shan State had evolved to a scale no one had anticipated.

Blasting around Bangkok in the back of a tuk tuk, my camera operator Sam Anderson and I were attempting to film what's known in TV as a piece to camera, where the reporter – me – tries to deliver a coherent sentence or two in front of the camera as a way of illustrating part of their story. In this case it was primarily happening as a way to capture some of the noise, colour and chaos of Bangkok – a visual antidote to the mind-numbingly dull conference centre where we'd spent all day monotonously filming world leaders repetitively shaking hands. We were there to cover Prime Minister Jacinda Ardern's attendance at Thailand's APEC summit, for *1News*, and as we whizzed past late-night food stands and street stalls packed with locals, the bars and cannabis shops selling booze and weed to locals and tourists alike, I was reporting how the big thrust for APEC 2022 was trying to get the region's economy pumping again after several years of stagnant growth and closed borders due to the Covid pandemic. In short, the message was 'we're open for business'.

The only problem with that, Jeremy Douglas had explained, was it also meant the region was once again open to the criminals and key players of the drug trade. They were flooding back into Thailand and the Golden Triangle as the borders reopened. Asia's not just a great place to go to the beach. Over the preceding few months, surveillance police from around the world watched as an influx of criminals they'd placed red flags on returned and they were now waiting for pre-Covid trafficking patterns to resume. It meant also expecting a whole lot more Myanmar meth to start moving, including heading Aotearoa's way.

Not that it wasn't coming in already.

At Auckland International Airport in early 2022, the police and Customs made what was then their biggest bust of meth at the border – 613 kilos of methamphetamine – packaged up in tea bags, the tell-tale sign that the drugs had come from the Golden Triangle. Police put the street value of the drugs at NZ$245 million and busted a bunch of people around Auckland with links to the Comancheros and Mongrel Mob gangs and began seizing their assets. As well as restraining a number of homes and freezing a bank account with one million dollars in it, the police hauled away gang members' Harley Davidson motorbikes, a Lamborghini Huracán and a Ferrari. They confiscated a 1968 Dodge Charger with a street value of $185,000 while they were at it for good measure too.

This may not have been their first shipment.

In late 2022 the Australian Federal Police incited controversy when they admitted to politicians at a Senate hearing that they were continuing to share meth-related intelligence with their Myanmar counterparts, despite the fact that the country was now ruled by a military junta that had arrested more than 15,000 thousand people, including a prominent Australian, and slaughtered several thousand pro-democracy activists. While slammed by some for sharing information with a police force that was committing vile human rights abuses, Australia's police commissioner defended it, saying testing still showed that 70 per cent of the methamphetamine on the streets of Australia had been cooked in Myanmar. I checked in with the New Zealand Police and Customs who insisted they haven't shared any meth-related intelligence with the Myanmar junta since just before the military coup in early 2021.

But other information-sharing between countries has been happening for a while. A few years ago, six Asian nations decided to team up and see if they could put a dent in meth production, launching 'Golden Triangle Operation 1511'. In 2020, this resulted in the operation seizing 450 million meth pills, more than 34 tonnes of crystal meth, 1 million kilos of precursor chemicals, while more than 16,000 people involved in the meth trade were arrested.

And the impact? The following year a new all-time record was set – more than a billion meth pills seized across Asia and around 80 tonnes of crystal. Because when it comes to synthetic drugs, seizing them doesn't really make any difference in the long run, or for that matter in the short, as the chemists can just cook more and replace their lost meth fast. It's got to the point where local governments in Southeast Asia are at a loss as to what to do about meth and the UN drugs body isn't even encouraging seizures anymore. Instead, it's advising governments to try to dismantle the traffickers' networks, disrupt their business – and you do that by restricting their access to the precursor chemicals they need and by targeting financial institutions to reduce their ability to move cash.

Bangkok-based drug expert Jeremy Douglas told me that the whole Asian drug scene had been flipped on its head over the last 10 to 15 years. While many Thai, Japanese and Filipino citizens had always had a big appetite for methamphetamine, most Asian nations were traditionally heroin markets and had been for decades. When it comes to the effects of meth versus heroin, they're worlds apart: meth is a powerful stimulant while heroin is a powerful nervous-system depressant.

First it was Cambodia, and then Laos, then one by one, countries all across Asia changed from favouring heroin to becoming meth markets, the whole region undergoing a radical and profound change, helped by local triads and other traffickers who adopted a market-saturation approach to methamphetamine in the region, flooding Asia with dirt-cheap meth mostly out of Myanmar.

On the streets of Bangkok you can buy a powerful methamphetamine pill known as ya ba for about US$1 a pill. Ya ba is around 20 per cent meth, the rest of the pill bulked up with a mix of high-intensity commercial caffeine, like they put in Red Bull, some binding agents and a little dye to make the pill pretty. In the north of Thailand, one ya ba costs 50 cents, much cheaper than beer, and is sought after by workers, and those looking to party. They're so widely available and so cheap now, they're easily accessible for anyone, even teens, with the price about a tenth of what it was just a few years ago.

The amount of methamphetamine being consumed in Thailand now 'is just insane', Douglas told me. In one year, in 2021, Thai authorities seized 600 million meth tablets that otherwise would have been consumed domestically, in a country with a population of 70 million. Thai health officials estimate there are 800,000 ya ba addicts.

The next time you hear some claim that New Zealand has the highest rate of meth use in the world, think 'yeah, nah', because it's just plain bullshit. Many nations where meth is by far and away the drug of choice simply don't conduct wastewater testing.

The Thai military has taken to sending soldiers into the heavily forested border areas with Myanmar and now regularly gun down smugglers bringing ya ba and ketamine into their country. In December 2022, it was reported they shot 15 men dead then posed for pictures with the corpses, and recovered 29 backpacks stuffed full of crystal meth. The month prior, four Thai monks in the northern province of Phetchabun made global news when they were evicted from their local temple after the police made them do urine tests and they all tested positive for methamphetamine.

The overwhelming focus in Asia remains on law enforcement, with most of the money available to combat meth in the region still spent on seizing drugs and making busts, whether they be users, couriers or occasionally someone higher up the chain. There's almost no focus on trying to stop people using meth by providing preventative education, and not much in the way of health services to help users minimise harm or get off the drug either.

Back in Afghanistan, the ceasefire between the United States and the Taliban in 2020 meant counter-narcotics operations in areas like Farah's meth-manufacturing Bakwa district effectively stopped completely as coalition forces prepared to depart the country in 2021. In the last days of the war, counter-narcotics officials warned that the country's diversification from opium into methamphetamine posed a possible catastrophe for the world. Not only was the Taliban already bringing in billions in revenue each year through the opium trade, it was now in the running for the title of the world's biggest drug cartel.

And while meth might be flowing out of Shan State and the Golden Triangle in record volumes, it is the inability for law enforcement, internationally, to stop the precursor chemicals used to manufacture the meth from flowing *into* these areas that is of major concern.

CHAPTER 5

CRYSTAL METH ACADEMY
The War on P

THE SOPHISTICATED DRUG NETWORKS ARE TWO STEPS AHEAD. And the people that governments and law enforcers are up against are very creative. They are innovators and problem solvers.

In Laos in July 2020 authorities stopped a suspicious-looking shipping container. Inside were blue drums filled with 72 tonnes of propionyl chloride that had been manufactured in China and were being sent to an area in northern Myanmar controlled by a militia known as the United Wa State Army – a militia accused of funding its activities through drug manufacturing. The authorities in Laos had never heard of propionyl chloride and it wasn't on the list of 30 precursor substances identified by the International Narcotics Control Board (which implements United Nations international drug control conventions). But after seeking advice from them, they found out it was a precursor chemical for both fentanyl and ephedrine.

The seizure was described as a smoking gun, proof of how drug syndicates use ingenious chemical engineering to get around the global restrictions on precursor chemicals needed to make meth. They now employ chemists to come up with their own designer precursors, or pre-precursors, relatively obscure chemicals, such as propionyl chloride, that aren't subject to international controls. They effectively create their own meth ingredients to be exported, piecemeal, to where the meth will be made.

And the outfoxing of authorities is clearly happening. In 2019, 325 tonnes of meth was seized globally – 43 per cent higher than the year before – and yet the total amount of controlled precursors that were seized in the same year could not have produced more than ten tonnes of meth.

It's the polar opposite of what was occurring less than ten years earlier when the precursors seized could have made 700 tonnes of meth, seven times greater than the actual 111 tonnes of meth captured.

The UNODC World Drug Report 2021 saw this as important, putting the difference down to a shift by drug syndicates to use non-controlled chemicals and their frequent changing up of meth-cooking methods too – to get around the much tighter controls on ephedrine and pseudoephedrine. For example, and bear with me as it gets a little technical, as soon as the chemical MAPA (methyl alpha-phenylacetoacetate), a pre-precursor used to cook meth using the P2P method, came under increasing scrutiny by law enforcements in 2020, traffickers immediately began showing an interest in EAPA (ethyl alpha-phenylacetoacetate), an analogue of MAPA. MAPA itself had only come to the attention of authorities in 2017 following a crackdown on another meth pre-precursor, APAA (alpha-phenylacetoacetamide). And around and around it goes.

China's Narcotics Control Commission openly acknowledges their country has a problem with its citizens setting up fly-by-night chemical companies to manufacture designer precursors for meth, which are then exported into the Golden Triangle or further afield.

The controversial US chemist-turned-author Steven Preisler, who wrote the infamous meth-cooking bible *Secrets of Methamphetamine Manufacture* under the nom de plume Uncle Fester while serving time in prison on meth charges, put it like this: 'chemical restrictions are like squeezing mud, the stuff just comes out between your fingers'.

Preisler said while restrictions may cause problems for people trying to cook meth at home, for those with connections it's not a problem. And he was talking about this back in 2009 when, following the crackdown on ephedrine and pseudoephedrine by the United States, Mexican cartels simply turned to the P2P method of cooking meth. This method had been used by US biker gangs and Preisler himself in the 1980s. It uses the chemical phenyl-2-propanone as a substitute for ephedrine to make meth, and while P2P itself was highly restricted, the chemicals required to make P2P could be found in huge quantities.

Restrictions on over-the-counter ephedrine and pseudo-ephedrine sales in the United States in 2005 did appear to be successful, initially, with domestic meth-manufacturing at the time still dominated by motorcycle gangs, whose members generally lacked the chemistry smarts to come up with alternative means of cooking it.

But it didn't take long for Mexican drug cartels to pick up the slack. The United States' Drug Enforcement Administration

(DEA) believes nearly all their main cartels are making and trafficking meth into the country – including, at last count, the Sinaloa Cartel, Jalisco New Generation Cartel, the Juárez Cartel, the Gulf Cartel, Los Zetas Cartel and the Beltrán-Leyva Organization.

In 2018, Mexican marines came across a meth super lab up in the mountains in Sinaloa state. The marines dug up scores of barrels of chemicals and more than 50 tonnes of crystal meth buried in pits, while a joint DEA and Mexican security forces operation the following year with heavily armed soldiers, backed up by .50-caliber guns mounted on armoured vehicles, came across another super lab in dense Sinaloa jungle. This one was capable of cooking seven tonnes of meth every three days – all of it destined for the United States market. 'What we saw in the jungles of Sinaloa was *Breaking Bad* on steroids,' US Marshal Nick Willard told the American press following the raid, his colleague noting it was just one of many Mexican meth labs.

Not only are Mexicans cooking lots of meth but the quality of their product has got phenomenally better, with the purity of their meth hitting 97 per cent in 2019; US officials claim the research and development capabilities of the drug cartels surpass those of Fortune 500 companies. Mexican chemists are so skilled at cooking meth using P2P now, they're highly sought after by criminal groups in other countries. Mexicans were involved in three meth super labs busted in 2019 in Belgium and the Netherlands, where the working theory is that they are helping local chemists hone their cooking skills.

In the Netherlands, the Dutch have been importing chemicals from China for decades to make amphetamines and ecstasy, which they then ship around the world. Their synthetic drug market was recently estimated to be worth around $30 billion. As police raided one barge in 2019 being used to cook meth, floating in a canal just outside of Rotterdam, the boat promptly began to sink – a pump had been activated that immediately spewed water into the vessel – but it wasn't fast enough. Along with three Mexican cooks, the police found 70 kilos of methamphetamine and a cartel-signature cooking process, which recycles what is normally waste product to make more meth. An experienced police officer described it thus: 'the crystal meth academy was now open in the Netherlands'.

Just over the border in Belgium, at a disused pig farm, three more Mexicans were caught, having just cooked up half a tonne of meth. In July 2020, Slovakian border authorities became suspicious of two large metal containers purportedly carrying liquids that had arrived via Croatia from Mexico, and when they drilled holes in the bottom, crystal meth began falling out: 1.5 tonnes of it. Announcing the bust, Slovakian authorities gave a special shout-out to their sniffer dog Hutch. In terms of illegal hauls, the size and value of this one simply had no precedent in their history. They estimated it had a street value of more than NZ$3 billion.

And early one evening in August 2021, another sniffer dog, this time at the Otay Mesa Port of Entry in San Diego, began to show extreme interest in a semi-trailer being driven across the border from Mexico by one Carlos Saavedra, a Mexican citizen. Preliminary checks indicated the presence of illegal narcotics, however, Saavedra was allowed to leave the port and was followed closely and kept under surveillance. When he parked the truck in a commercial lot, left the keys under the hood and began walking away, he only made it about 100 metres before being arrested. Agents thoroughly searched the truck. They found 400 packages of meth, weighing a total of 2.5 tonnes, along with 52 kilos of fentanyl. It was one of the biggest meth busts in US history according to DEA Special Agent John Callery, who described it as not only a blow to the cartels but also a victory against the meth and fentanyl overdosing that was plaguing the United States.

Just three weeks later, at the start of September, South Korea made its biggest meth bust: more than 400 kilos of Mexican meth was found inside helical gears – a circular-shaped machine part often used in aircraft – but officials say it was bound for Australia, and they feared another 500 kilos had already made it Down Under.

While law enforcement may celebrate the occasional bust, Mexico's meth industry is now breaking meth seizure records on a monthly basis, and that's just the meth that gets stopped. At some of San Diego's bustling border crossings, agents are said to have around 40 seconds to decide whether a vehicle is suspicious, whether it be because of a nervous driver or passengers, custom-made compartments or unusually weighed-down vehicles. And the drugs don't just come over the border, they come under it too. Local law enforcement in San Diego have a dedicated Tunnel Task Force, which tracks down tunnels that run from Mexico and pop up in the factories of commercial areas in San Diego border towns.

In one bust in early 2020, the task force uncovered a 600-metre-long tunnel from Tijuana, Mexico into a factory in Otay Mesa – the tunnel was a metre wide, and ten metres below ground, complete with ventilation, reinforced walls and an underground rail system. Inside was an Aladdin's cave of drugs including 1300 kilos of marijuana, 600 kilos of cocaine, 39 kilos of meth, 7 kilos of heroin and a kilo of fentanyl to boot. It was a $45 million seizure and the first time five different narcotics had been discovered in the same tunnel. A few months earlier, they'd uncovered the longest tunnel they'd ever found at 1.3 kilometres in length, and while no drugs were found, the cops noted that as they increased security at the borders above ground, the sophisticated subterranean efforts of the Mexican cartels were increasing.

While vast quantities of meth are being trafficked into the United States, just like what occurred in New Zealand, the amount of meth being cooked domestically there is falling fast. Fewer than 900 labs were busted in the US in 2019, and nearly all of them were small scale 'kitchen labs' capable of producing just a few ounces per cook – fifteen years earlier in 2004 US cops raided almost 24,000 of them The number of super labs being busted there – ones that can produce around 5 kilos of meth per cook – also plunged from 245 in 2001 to just 11 in 2018.

There's clearly still some demand for clan meth labs though, particularly as traffickers turn to liquid meth to try to outwit authorities.

Sniffer dogs on duty with Mexican navy inspectors at the port of Manzanillo in April 2023 alerted them to more than 11,000 tequila bottles that contained enough liquid meth to make more than eight tonnes of the drug and were destined for export.

When liquid meth shipments do successfully deceive authorities and make it to their destination, they get taken to labs where the water is extracted and the meth turned into its crystal form.

In the four years between 2015 and 2019, 23,000 meth labs were busted and dismantled by law enforcement globally, but the numbers being found is plummeting too; from more than 10,000 in 2010 to just 1600 in 2019. There's a clear trend towards far fewer labs, cooking vastly greater amounts of meth.

These trends are also reflected in the New Zealand market. A couple of years ago, New Zealand's border agencies identified the top three countries of concern when it came to trafficking meth to New Zealand: Thailand was in top place (authorities seized nearly 500 kilos of meth that had left that country in 2019); United States in second place, with nearly 200 kilos; then Mexico, with 160 kilograms. And while meth may have left from Thailand and the United States for our shores, Myanmar and Mexico are where the P was cooked.

Operating as markets do, the increased supply and competition from global meth producers saw the price of a kilo of meth fall in New Zealand from $250,000 in 2016 to $150,000 just three years later.

* * *

When Oklahoma Highway Patrol state trooper Shiloh Hall pulled over a speeding SUV in Okmulgee County shortly after midnight one April night in 2012, he noticed an unusual chemical smell wafting from the vehicle. And as the trooper began to question the vehicle's occupants about said smell, the 54-year-old passenger David Williams decided it was time to leg it, and so began a very brief foot pursuit, followed by an equally brief struggle. It was during that altercation that the miniature meth lab Williams had stuffed down the leg of his pants burst and he soon found himself not only sitting in handcuffs but soaked in meth too.

A small-scale recipe for cooking meth was booming in popularity across North America, and just one trip to the discount department store Walmart was enough to secure almost everything you needed to make a small batch using the shake'n'bake one pot method.

First up you'd need a sturdy plastic bottle (Gatorade or plastic SodaStream bottles were favoured vessels), then you'd round up some commonly available items, and the key ingredient – some Sudafed or other pseudoephedrine-based cold and flu tablets – and you were well on your way to cooking your own meth.

You'd go through a process of mixing the chemicals, shaking and heating and burping your bottle, and with a little practice by the end you'd be left with between one and two grams of crystal methamphetamine.

A couple of years after Williams made national headlines for being the man who had a meth lab explode in his pants, a high school science class in New Hampshire was learning about tree identification in some local woods when they came across a two-litre plastic bottle that was bubbling, contracting and expanding all of its own accord.

Their science teacher carried the bottle back into the school building in order to secure it, not appreciating how volatile it was. After realising that probably wasn't the best of ideas she placed it outside, at which time it promptly burst into flames.

While you can make a little meth in a Gatorade bottle, you can literally make tonnes in a super-lab, and when *National Geographic* was given a tour of one such cartel meth lab in a Mexican jungle, the site was filled with gas bottles, plastic barrels filled with fuel and sack after sack of chemicals like lead and what the cartel's men called 'cookie' — a mix of other ingredients that would then be heated in large cauldrons. By the end of the process they were producing meth with a purity in the high 90s. As *National Geographic* reporter Mariana van Zeller explained, labs like this are making meth on an industrial scale.

In Aotearoa much of our meth manufacturing is done in labs that are rather rudimentary affairs. Relatively small-scale batches are cooked up on kitchen bench-tops, or in sheds and garages which are littered with beakers, plastic tubes, glass jars and bottles full of acid.

As Detective Sergeant Rhys Wilson of the National Clan Lab Response unit once explained to a reporter, it was very rare for his team to ever come across anything that looked as sophisticated as a science laboratory, the reality is that many kiwi meth labs are pretty ad-hoc.

Most of those doing the cooking were no chemistry wizards either, he added, just jokers who'd copied recipes from their mates.

* * *

While Mexican cartels, ruthless and ingenious in equal measure, are grabbing a bigger slice of the world's meth market, it was the arrest of the leader of a Chinese drug syndicate known as The Company, or the Sam Gor Syndicate, by authorities, in Amsterdam in 2021 that led to police departments celebrating around the world. The Company was headed by Tse Chi Lop, a Canadian citizen in his late fifties who was born in China and has been likened to both El Chapo and Pablo Escobar because of the scale of his operations.

He was Asia's most wanted man and said to be protected around the clock by a team of elite Thai kickboxers and accused of running one of the main syndicates helping to produce and distribute the meth being made in Myanmar's Shan State super labs. Part of Tse Chi Lop's success was that The Company had managed to unite five of Asia's major triad groups, all in the pursuit of profit. One estimate had the syndicate pulling in up to NZ$24 billion a year from meth alone, and it was thought to be exporting meth to more than a dozen countries, from Japan to New Zealand.

The Company excelled at connecting suppliers and distributors across the world, and even those who spend their time fighting global drug networks were in awe of its ability to broker major deals. Their forte was getting various criminal groups, internationally, to cooperate, and in doing so were able to move untold tonnes of crystal meth out of the Golden Triangle and to their customers all around the world. They were known for concealing the meth in packets of tea, while some estimates had The Company controlling around half of the entire meth trade in the Asia-Pacific region.

Australian Federal Police in particular had been hunting Tse Chi Lop for more than a decade, believing him to be one of the world's most successful meth masterminds, alleging he had orchestrated huge shipments of meth into their country. When an inspection of a shipping container at a Melbourne port in 2019 led to Australia's biggest meth bust, intercepting 1.6 tonnes of meth hidden inside stereo speakers, it was all wrapped in green-tea packaging, the Sam Gor signature. The ship had departed Bangkok, Thailand, but the meth had originated from Myanmar.

Dutch police arrested Tse Chi Lop at Schipol Airport in Amsterdam in January 2021 as he was boarding a flight to Canada and prepared to deport him. He appealed his extradition, claiming his arrest was illegal and accusing Australian authorities of arranging for his expulsion from Taiwan to Canada to include a stopover in the Netherlands so that he would be arrested there. In New Zealand, news of the arrest was welcomed by Detective Superintendent Greg Williams, who said The Company was behind some of the biggest meth shipments into our country and his capture was evidence that no one was untouchable. A United Nations drug official said the importance of Tse's arrest could not be underestimated.

In December 2022, Tse Chi Lop landed in Australia and was taken straight to the Melbourne Magistrates' Court, where he appeared on charges of conspiracy to traffic commercial quantities of methamphetamine into Australia. If found guilty, he faces life in prison.

* * *

Kiwi soldiers came face to face with German paratroopers fuelled by meth, such as these during the invasion of Suda Bay, Crete, on 20 May 1941. *(Australian War Memorial, P00433.009)*

Above: 'Pervitin' was an over-the-counter methamphetamine tablet used by the German military during the Second World War. *(Wikimedia Commons)*

Left: Organic chemist Nagayoshi Nagai, the 'father of meth', extracted the methamphetamine-precursor drug ephedrine from the ephedra plant well over 100 years ago. *(Wikimedia Commons)*

Amphetamines were available at all good chemists not long ago, while methamphetamine was liberally prescribed for weight loss.

A jazz pianist in the 1950s playing under the influence of Benzedrine. 'Bennies' were a popular amphetamine stimulant. *(Vecchio/Three Lions/Getty Images)*

Markets may have changed but disposal methods haven't.

Above: Detectives in Harrisburg, Pennsylvania, in the 1960s pour 15,000 'pep pills' into the city incinerator after a bust. *(Bettman via Getty Images)*

Below: Police taking part in Operation Thunder raid Boshe Village, Guangdong Province, China, in December 2013, and cart away close to 30 tonnes of meth, ketamine and precursor chemicals. Security forces arrested over 180 locals and dismantled 77 meth labs. In the narrow alleys of 'The Fortress', China's number-one meth-making village, locals formed roadblocks and used rocks, homemade grenades, firearms and crossbows in attempts to repel them. *(Reuters/Stringer)*

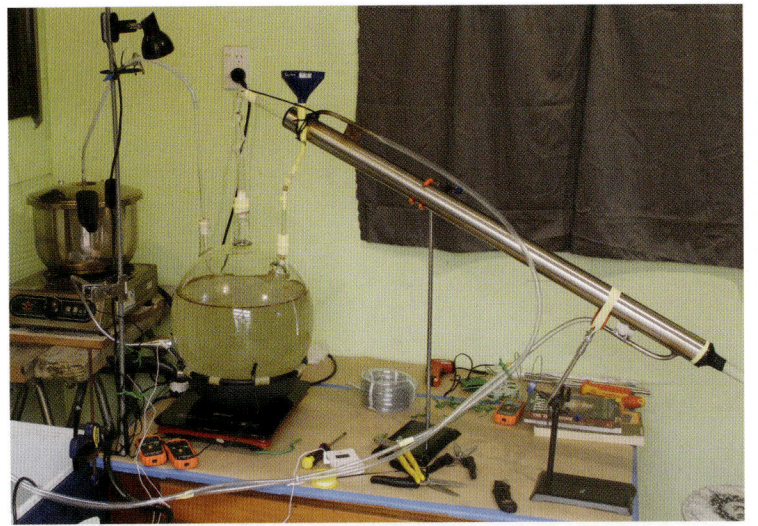

As recipes for cooking meth spread in New Zealand, so too did clan meth labs like these. Police say Kiwi meth labs are often ramshackle affairs.
(Courtesy NZ Police)

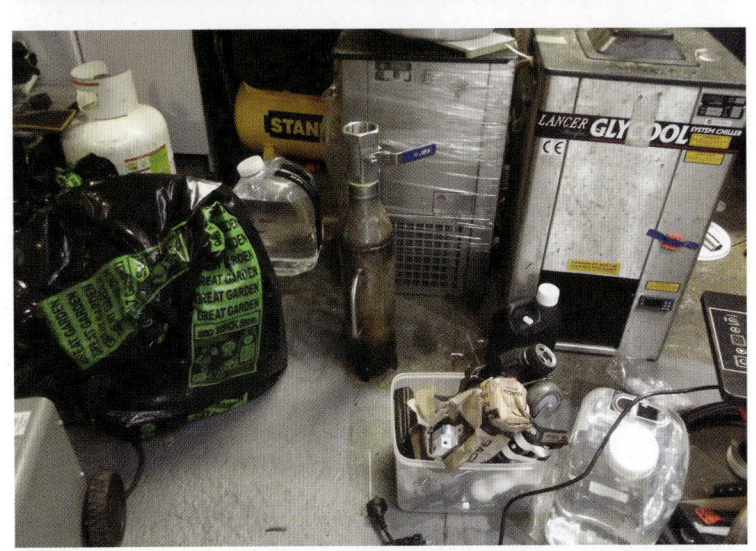

A lonely memorial by Lake Ōnoke in South Wairarapa, to 'treasured girl' six-year-old Coral Ellen Burrows, who was murdered in a fit of meth-induced paranoid rage by her stepfather, Steven Williams, in 2003. The ripples of meth manufacture are felt far from the Golden Triangle and Mexican jungles, even in quiet villages like Lake Ferry.

Coral Ellen Burrows
10.03.1997 - 09.09.2003
The place of our treasured girl.
Forever in our hearts.

'When they go high, we go low.' Mexican drug smugglers try to outfox the US authorities with elaborate drug-smuggling tunnels beneath the US–Mexico border. *(Courtesy US Attorney's Office, Southern District of California)*

Relatives mourn at the funeral of drug runner Leah Espiritu, in the Philippines, 11 June 2017. Espiritu was killed by unknown assailants who were presumed to be undercover police or part of state-sanctioned death squads. *(Ezra Acayan/NurPhoto via Getty Images)*

The mother of a victim killed by vigilante death squads in the Philippines poses with a mock body of her son, hoping the publicity will help highlight the horror of her government's extrajudicial killings of 'shabu' (meth) users. *(J Gerard Seguia/SOPA Images/LightRocket via Getty Images)*

New Zealand Prime Minister Jacinda Ardern (fifth from left) awkwardly holds hands with the Philippines' President Rodrigo 'The Punisher' Duterte in 2019. Duterte publicly urged and celebrated the slaughter of shabu users, promising 'the fish in Manila Bay would grow fat feeding on their corpses'. *(Manan Vatsyayana, AFP via Gettty Images)*

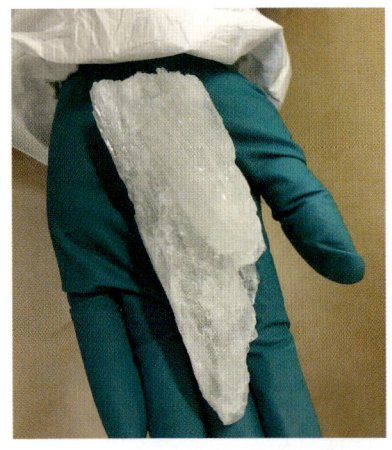

Ordering in. Trained professional chemists now manufacture high-quality methamphetamine in super labs abroad before it is shipped to New Zealand. *(Courtesy NZ Customs)*

Meth is smuggled into the country every which way. Customs show off this haul they detected inside golf-cart batteries in 2019. *(Courtesy NZ Customs)*

Tse Chi Lop, the alleged mastermind behind the global meth-trafficking syndicate The Company, is taken into custody in Australia in December 2022. The Company shipped meth by the tonne. *(Courtesy Australian Federal Police)*

This maple syrup was not so sweet. New Zealand authorities found around three-quarters of a tonne of methamphetamine hidden inside bottles such as these in Auckland, 2023. *(Courtesy NZ Customs)*

Before embarking on a drug run in Mexico, it's been said traffickers will often pray to their unofficial saint Jesús Malverde to request good fortune and a little assistance from on high to evade the authorities and make a successful delivery. Jesús Malverde was originally revered as a Robin Hood-like figure, a bandit from Sinaloa, Mexico, who stole from the rich and gave to the poor, but folklore has it that in the 1970s, a drug trafficker who had been shot by his own father and thrown into the sea miraculously survived after praying to Malverde while floating in the ocean. This led to him becoming worshipped as a narco-saint.

And Waikato man Kerry Murphy may well have felt there had been some divine intervention when, during his 2011 methamphetamine case in the High Court, all drug charges against him were thrown out. Two years earlier he'd been caught red-handed by police officers with nearly 1.7 kilos of methamphetamine when they raided his Morrinsville home, but in a stroke of what appeared to unbelievably good luck for Murphy, the cops involved in the raid seriously misled the judge about the circumstances of the raid, which in turn led to a ruling that all their evidence was inadmissible. Explaining his decision, the judge said that while there was almost no doubt that Murphy and his co-accused were serious drug offenders, and while he realised that this ruling would quite possibly leave the public dismayed, there were wider legal issues at stake. The charges were dropped and Murphy was free to go.

But it didn't take long for his good luck to run out. In October the following year, the police were led by a concerned associate of Murphy's to an abandoned mineshaft deep in the bush not far from the Coromandel town of Whitianga, where they found chemicals and equipment and a rugged DIY methamphetamine laboratory – and the bodies of two local P cooks, Murphy and Grant 'Grunty' Wyllie. The men, both in their forties, had been powering their P lab with a petrol generator but had died from accidental carbon monoxide poisoning when the wind changed and the fumes blew into the mineshaft and overwhelmed them. The senior police officer at the Thames Coromandel CIB, Ross Patterson, warned that the double tragedy showed both the risks of operating petrol-powered engines in confined spaces and the dangers of dabbling with meth manufacturing.

They weren't the first New Zealanders to die accidentally while cooking meth. A few years earlier, two men had been badly burnt in a meth-lab fire near Wellsford, one of them fatally. Residents on Mt Maunganui's prestigious Oceanbeach Road were woken by the police knocking on their doors early one morning in 2013 asking them to evacuate as the meth lab their neighbour had been operating in his basement exploded. 'This is supposed to be one of the top addresses in New Zealand to live. Then we have something like this; it's quite bizarre,' one affected neighbour told their local paper. It was clear that meth could be cooked anywhere.

But for every dramatic meth lab explosion and fire that gained national attention, there were dozens and dozens of run-of-the-mill busts, where specialists wearing protective clothing and breathing apparatus would be brought in to dismantle the set-up, to ensure no one was harmed by the array of chemicals involved.

And while all of this is a far cry from the super-labs of Myanmar and the infamous drug cartels in Mexico, these Kiwi household meth labs became a grave concern in New Zealand as more and more of them sprouted. They were thought to pose a huge threat to people's health and caused major damage, and inflicted massive costs, financially and emotionally, on all involved, whether intentionally or not. This scandal is what we now need to address.

CHAPTER 6

MORAL PANIC
A New Threat for Homeowners, Landlords and Government Tenants

WHILE THE NUMBER OF METH LABS BEING BUSTED STARTED to decline in the new millennium, especially following the banning of pseudoephedrine-based cold medicines, in 2009 New Zealanders were told a new threat to people's health was emerging: the contamination of homes from P. Scientists and health officials got together and came up with a set of guidelines for cleaning houses that had been used as meth labs – to ensure they were safe for people to live in again. And the scale of the problem was thought to be huge.

Headlines like this from *The New Zealand Herald* in March 2016 were common: 'It's feared P-riddled homes could rival NZ's leaky homes disaster, with thousands thought to be contaminated'.

Housing New Zealand (HNZ, now Kāinga Ora), was warning that hundreds of its homes were being ruined by meth contamination; by 2015, statistics showed as many as 600 state homes would need to be decontaminated, costing taxpayers millions of dollars. And things were just as bad, if not worse, for private landlords when it came to their investment rental properties.

One prominent meth-testing company, MethSolutions, reported the same year that 40 per cent of the 400 homes they had tested recently in the Waikato region had come back positive for methamphetamine. The company's director, Miles Stratford, reported that children were regularly becoming sick from P contamination in their homes. In fact, the kids were effectively 'running around on low doses of methamphetamine themselves', Stratford told reporters, and they were often the first to show side effects of skin rashes, eye irritability, sleeplessness and headaches. Their unsuspecting parents might notice that their children weren't well, he continued, but they didn't think to have their homes tested for meth, and it was only when they finally did that they realised meth was the cause of little Johnny's illness all along. Owners of commercial properties must stay alert too, Stratford warned. If a warehouse or site has power and water, it could be turned into a clandestine lab.

Meanwhile, another drug-testing company was warning that the use of methamphetamine was 'booming' in the country; not only were teenagers getting hooked on the insidious drug but so too were retirees! And hair follicle samples showed children as young as ten were testing positive for meth, simply from living in these homes. The risks posed to children living in a house with methamphetamine residue was a major talking point everywhere. Media articles on meth were frequently accompanied by 'The problem with P' factsheets. These 'facts' warned that toddlers only needed to be crawling on contaminated carpet to potentially suffer from neurological damage or kidney failure, while high exposure could cause severe lung or throat damage, or even death.

Meth-cleaning company Envirocheck told the media in 2016 that up to 20 per cent of Kiwi homes were contaminated by methamphetamine. Envirocheck's boss, David Kilburn, said 'naive homeowners' were often being caught out, thinking that just because they were buying their new home from an elderly couple who had lived there for 20 years, there was no need to carry out meth testing, only to discover later that the home was in fact contaminated with P. He said people needed to ask themselves if they could vouch for every guest who had been to that elderly couple's home? Had they ever had their grandchildren over to stay? Could one of those grandchildren be a meth head?

It was all too clear to homeowners, and people looking to become one, that meth residue posed a significant threat to their health, that contamination of properties was way too common and no one, from retirees to grandchildren, could be ruled out as potential suspects. The only way to keep everyone safe was to get their property meth-tested by one of the scores of companies that had popped up offering such services.

Even major insurance company AMI came on board, warning people they should never assume their property was safe from meth contamination, given the drug was so widely used. As luck would have it, AMI also offered to sell homeowners an array of insurance policies, covering possible meth contamination of their home or rental property – and even their car.

And this is the way the meth testing rolled for years, with those profiting from this new industry never missing a media opportunity to air their shocking claims, until there was a change of government in late 2017. Pretty much the first thing the new housing minister, Phil Twyford, did was order an official investigation into it. But before then, so many lives were upended and so much unjustified expense inflicted.

*　*　*

When Beka and Derek Radford decided to rent out their hardy three-bedroom house in Hamilton in May 2015 while they went to the UK for their big OE, the young couple happily shelled-out $300 for basic meth-testing before their first tenant moved in so they could reassure both the tenant and themselves that their home was P-free.

At that time, everywhere they looked, meth contamination was in the news, and not only that but they'd had a good friend who had been caught out after buying a home without getting a meth test done first, only to discover later that there was indeed contamination. And the head of the Tenancy Tribunal, Melissa Poole, was warning property investors that 'any trace of meth was too high', even if those levels were below current standards set out by the Ministry of Health. The tribunal was awarding penalties in the tens of thousands of dollars against both statehouse tenants and renters in the private market when just a few millionths of a gram of meth was detected on a surface, holding them liable for the full cost of decontaminating their former abodes.

When Beka and Derek returned to New Zealand in 2017, they asked their tenants to move on after a dispute over a dog on the property, and decided to spruce their house up with the intention of renting it out to help pay the costs while relocating to Auckland. They'd just began repainting when they made the decision to get the house retested for meth – not that they had any suspicions about their previous tenants; they just wanted to be on the safe side. And much to their dismay, in November that year, the tests came back showing traces of meth in multiple rooms, with the bathroom and laundry area recording by far the highest reading in the house, of 6.6 micrograms of meth. They were immediately advised by the meth-testing company that their health was at extreme risk and they were likely to become sick just from being in the home. Their former tenants meanwhile denied ever touching the drug and blamed it on a friend of theirs who had briefly house-sat the property.

Derek and Beka felt they didn't have a choice but to have the house decontaminated. With both starting new jobs in Auckland, they couldn't afford their rent there while also paying their Hamilton mortgage and they were aware of Tenancy Tribunal cases where tenants had taken cases against their landlords for renting out meth-contaminated homes. So, they couldn't rent it out, and they couldn't sell it because prospective buyers would no doubt carry out meth tests too, so they simply had to fix it.

The distraught young couple booked a professional meth-cleaning company, which Beka told me involved the company basically waterblasting the inside of the home and using shit tonnes of sugar soap to reduce the meth levels and causing a shit tonne of water damage in the process.

On the advice of the company, their carpets were ripped out, skirting boards and kitchen benchtops removed, their heat pump had to be biffed as did all their curtains and light shades – even their electrical outlets had to go. Meth, they were told, really likes to settle on plastic.

With their house now decontaminated and gutted, Beka project managed the builders and other tradies to fix it. Not only that but they began a fight with AMI insurance over the $40,000 clean-up bill that threatened to bankrupt them (they did eventually win the battle, with their insurer covering a lot of the damage). The whole thing left Beka traumatised and requiring several weeks off work due to the stress. And Beka and Derek were just one couple of many caught up in the growing public panic about meth contamination.

Meanwhile, HNZ was ramping up the use of meth testing on its properties, and finding a significant number of them with traces of P as a result. The agency, whose job it is to house vulnerable New Zealanders, developed a zero-tolerance approach for dealing with those it deemed responsible for meth contamination and began publicly celebrating the enormous costs being awarded against the tenants it accused of contaminating their properties. In one case, in Ashburton, a tenant was evicted and then fined $34,000 by the Tenancy Tribunal for P contamination.

Housing New Zealand's chief operating officer Paul Commons was almost ecstatic as he issued a media statement saying this decision not only reinforced his agency's determination not to take a backward step in fighting meth contamination but also that it sent a strong message to their tenants that their tenancies would be swiftly terminated should they engage in criminal activity such as using meth in their homes. Not only that, the agency would also pursue the tenants accused of contaminating their homes for the cost of the clean-up and blacklist them from moving into another state house for at least 12 months. By 2016, in the middle of a housing crisis, there were hundreds of state homes sitting empty because of meth contamination.

'Babies living in P-contaminated houses' was the headline of one *New Zealand Herald* article that year, which revealed that multiple state-housing tenants, mostly solo mums, were being evicted from a social housing development in Christchurch after their homes tested positive for meth. Toddlers and infants had been found living there and Social Housing Minister Paula Bennett said she was particularly distressed by the incident given the age of the 'wee babies' involved.

Even more distressing were the cases of children taken from their parents once their home had tested positive for methamphetamine.

More hype continued. An episode of TVNZ's *Fair Go*, which was looking into the contamination issue, collected bank notes from dairies and shops around Auckland and sent them off for meth testing. Every single note came back with traces of methamphetamine, and some of the bank notes had higher levels of meth found on them than the level at which state-housing tenants were being evicted. This led the *Fair Go* reporter to quip that 'there might be more P in your pocket than there is on your walls'.

I was working as a journalist for Radio New Zealand in the press gallery at Parliament in Wellington at the time, and using the Official Information Act, I obtained the actual test results for that home in Ashburton where the tenant had been evicted and stung for $34,000 – the penalty that public servants at Housing New Zealand had rushed to welcome. I also called a senior lecturer in environmental chemistry at Massey University, Dr Nick Kim, to discuss this with him. He began questioning the science on which Housing New Zealand was basing its evictions. He said the levels of meth contamination were so low in the Ashburton house he couldn't even be sure anyone had used the drug there.

Dr Kim was concerned that people were being evicted from their homes for forensic-level traces of a drug residue that was known to be found in higher concentrations on money that people carried around with them, which he pointed out could clearly be a possible source of contamination. He felt the whole meth-testing 'craze' and the evictions and punishments that followed was bordering on the bizarre. He also explained what he saw as the major flaw with the meth testing being carried out: the meth-testing companies, HNZ and the Tenancy Tribunal were using the Ministry of Health's 2010 Guidelines for the Remediation of Clandestine Methamphetamine Laboratory Sites as the golden rulebook for determining contamination.

These guidelines warned that during the meth-cooking process, toxic chemicals used during manufacturing could become airborne and settle on walls, carpets and floors, possibly posing a risk to any people in the house. Methamphetamine was the chemical used as the gauge or marker chemical. If you could clean the area up and get the level of meth down to 0.5 micrograms per 100 centimetres squared, then the other chemicals around would be at such low levels they couldn't cause any harm and the site would be safe to reoccupy. But it was never intended for the guidelines to be used to evict people from their homes, Dr Kim said, they were a guide for reoccupying homes that had previously been used to cook methamphetamine – and he was well placed to comment; he was involved in developing the guidelines with the Ministry of Health in the first place.

In a separate interview with the New Zealand Drug Foundation, Kim reiterated that the 0.5 microgram value was incredibly, incredibly low, and around 2000 times lower than a single typical daily dose of methamphetamine given to a child with ADHD as a medicine – and yet houses were being declared uninhabitable at this level.

A microgram is one millionth of a gram.

But the biggest problem of all with this whole issue, he told me, was that nearly all of the meth testing was taking place in homes that had never been meth labs at all. In fact, in the vast majority of homes being decontaminated, where tenants were being evicted and punished, and where landlords were financially crippled by decontamination costs, meth had only ever been smoked there, if it had been used at all. The guidelines were never designed to judge the danger of residues from smoking meth, while the toxic chemicals used in manufacturing meth in the early 2000s had simply never been present in these homes.

In August 2016, I interviewed Housing New Zealand's chemical contamination manager, Charlie Mitchell, about its meth-testing programme and the evictions. While he conceded that meth-lab guidelines were not entirely suitable for evicting people from their state homes where only meth use was suspected, he argued that the agency's zero tolerance for illegal behaviour trumped any shortfalls in the science. He was adamant that, if Housing New Zealand detected meth in a house, they would terminate the tenancy and pursue the tenant for costs. The argument seemed to be that there was no real difference between a former meth lab and a house in which P has been smoked.

To hell with the science.

And that viewpoint went all the way to the top. Housing Minister Bill English said while the guidelines were obviously not fit for purpose, the evictions would continue because those at Housing New Zealand were not scientists and simply could not just 'wish away' the meth-lab guidelines.

Yet there was definitely growing public concern that the meth-testing industry, the National government and the HNZ officials were out of control.

The Māngere Budgeting Services Trust, a social agency that helps those in need in their community with everything from providing food parcels and running cooking classes to counselling and advocating for housing rights, told me that people in South Auckland were living in fear of being falsely accused of contaminating their homes with meth. They said it was simply unfair that Housing New Zealand was refusing to test houses in between tenancies, something known as a 'baseline test', and even though tenancies changed frequently, with people moving in and out the traces of meth would stay behind. They were aware of multiple cases of families in their area who had never had anything to do with drugs, who were being falsely accused by the housing department. They also fairly pointed out, when state-housing tenants deny accusations made by the government, they seldom come out on top.

Dame Tariana Turia, a former Member of Parliament, had a story of her own about meth testing that she shared with me. In 2016, some close family friends of hers had held a twenty-first birthday party at their state house, and by her own admission it was fairly riotous – pretty much anything could have taken place there. Whether it was sparked by complaints from neighbours about the party isn't clear, but not long after, Housing New Zealand sent in the meth testers, and when the results came back positive, her friends' lives were turned upside down.

Despite the baseline test for meth having not been carried out before they moved into the property, her friends were held accountable for the contamination, and not only were they evicted from their home but also HNZ informed Children's Services, who removed their two kids from their parents. The detection of a few millionths of a gram of methamphetamine in a house was now justification for the state breaking up a family.

The government repeatedly said it had no alternative but to use the Ministry of Health's meth-lab remediation guidelines to police the use of meth. I approached the Ministry's media team for an interview, and as is their custom, was promptly refused. But in a stroke of good fortune, I managed to find a home phone number for their director of regulation and assurance. To my great surprise, Dr Stewart Jessamine picked up and was happy to be interviewed. He told me that the Ministry of Health had repeatedly raised its concerns with HNZ about how they were using, or rather, misusing the meth guidelines. He said it was blatantly clear the guidelines were only for use in houses where methamphetamine had been manufactured.

In this world of government agencies, I was aware how extraordinary it was to hear one effectively accuse another of misconduct – and it ignited a political firestorm. Housing New Zealand was labelled deplorable by the Green Party, and accused of a staggering level of incompetence by Labour, which said the agency had been caught up in the grips of a moral panic. The Drug Foundation weighed in too. Its director, Ross Bell, had long argued that meth testing was a scam run by 'an industry full of cowboys' and he now accused HNZ of deliberately evicting and blacklisting vulnerable tenants when they knew all along what they were doing was wrong.

There was one big question following this story, he said: 'What the hell are Housing New Zealand going to do now?'

And what did it do? It doubled down.

The media company Stuff ran an opinion piece for Housing New Zealand, in which COO Paul Commons attacked my coverage of their misuse of meth-lab guidelines and argued everyone else was mistaken. He said they had never misused them, they had never been accused of misusing them, they'd never split up families – although he admitted they did alert welfare agencies, who did split them.

Housing New Zealand continued to carry out meth tests, continued to refuse to conduct baseline tests and continued to evict its tenants, despite the objections from social agencies, and proof from scientists, including those who had helped write the meth-testing guidelines. At a select committee hearing at Parliament in 2017, HNZ boss Andrew McKenzie again accused the media of being wrong about it all, and then scuttled away from journalists before we could ask any questions.

It was just a few months later that the house I was trying to buy in Cannons Creek, Porirua tested positive for methamphetamine. Looking back on it all now, I wonder why I hesitated for a second in declining to pay for those meth tests. But it wouldn't be long before I knew I'd made the right call.

* * *

In late 2017, with Labour now in power, Housing Minister Phil Twyford began the official investigation into the meth-testing industry. And once again the government turned to the Prime Minister's chief science advisor, Sir Peter Gluckman. Half a year later Gluckman and his colleague Dr Anne Bardsley (now deputy director of Koi Tū: The Centre for Informed Futures) released their report. They believed that New Zealand was in the grips of 'a groundless moral panic'. They shot down the meth-testing industry that had sprung up in the country, saying they found no evidence in the international medical literature or from talking to experts of anyone being harmed by passive exposure to meth at any level.

Gluckman said the meth-testing industry made no sense, and he couldn't figure out the leap in logic that had seen the standards for cleaning up old-style meth labs end up being applied to homes where the drug had only been smoked. The Gluckman report found New Zealand was unique in developing a meth-testing industry that focused on the smoking of the drug, whereas in other nations the focus was solely on former meth labs. What's more, he said, toxic compounds such as lead and mercury that had been used in clan meth labs overseas had never been found in Aotearoa.

Further, P manufacture in New Zealand had evolved to the extent that most commonly used methods no longer emitted harmful solvents and the only contaminant really being emitted anymore was methamphetamine itself. Mould, a common feature in many Kiwi homes, was vastly more dangerous to people's health, they reported.

Gluckman's advice to homeowners thinking about getting a meth test: don't even bother. There was simply no point unless the police had advised you that the property was a former meth lab, and he recommended a much higher testing benchmark of 15 micrograms per 100 cm^2 be adopted.

As for those worried about infants, or 'the wee babies' who might come into contact with meth residue, this new limit came with a 1000–10,000-fold safety factor, he told the media. As he described it, a naked toddler could crawl around on the floor for several hours licking up every bit of carpet, at 15 micrograms per 100 cm^2, and not be harmed.

The report backed the concerns voiced by some in the media and scientists and the apologies started flowing thick and fast. Phil Twyford apologised for the appalling treatment people had suffered at the hands of his agency; National's new leader, Simon Bridges, was sorry that the advice they'd received while in government was incorrect. At a press conference following the report's release, Housing New Zealand's Andrew McKenzie, now sitting next to his new political master, finally saw fit to apologise and admit they'd been wrong all along, saying he really regretted the way it had all played out under his watch.

A subsequent investigation ordered by Twyford found that around 800 tenants and their families, including about 1500 children, had been wrongfully evicted. It found that in many cases the tenants had had their personal possessions destroyed by HNZ, which deemed them to be contaminated by meth, and in the worst cases, people were made homeless. The average compensation paid out was a little under $8000, which was probably more appreciated than the formal apology they also received from HNZ. And the millions of dollars of debt the state-house tenants had incurred for decontamination costs were also wiped.

One noticeable absentee when the apologies were being delivered was Housing New Zealand's chair, Adrienne Young-Cooper. Instead of fronting up to say sorry for the damage and harm her agency had inflicted, she took an overseas holiday. And what's also interesting, while HNZ had ignored the warnings, wasted taxpayers' money and its overzealous officials harmed many of its vulnerable tenants, no one at Housing New Zealand lost their job. You've got to wonder what was the point of it all.

The government issued an apology to landlords and homeowners across the country who they said had been duped by the meth-testing industry, which had exploited people and showed a lack of clear guidelines around meth testing. But it ruled out any compensation for those in the private sector. Prime Minister Jacinda Ardern said there was simply never any mandatory requirement for anyone to get their homes meth-tested in the first place.

The Gluckman report was a death blow for many companies in the meth-testing industry. The following year, journalist Susan Edmunds interviewed Miles Stratford of MethSolutions. The business had halved since the release of the report. Photographed sitting in a now bare office, he fumed at what he believed was an orchestrated campaign by vested interests to take down the meth-testing industry. If the Government can do this to their industry, he warned, they can do it to others.

Before the Gluckman report, it was estimated a meth test had been a precondition for around 30 per cent of house sales; now it had fallen to about 3 per cent and about 100 meth-testing and remediation businesses had shut up shop, Edmunds reported. The meth-testers had become pariahs.

When asked about the industry's demise, Dr Anne Bardsley didn't feel sorry for them. She said they'd brought it upon themselves by the way they'd behaved with their scaremongering and false statements about the risks of meth contamination. You just can't get sick from a few millionths of a gram of methamphetamine that's stuck to a surface or an extractor fan because 'it's not volatile, it doesn't come off the walls', Bardsley said.

Unfortunately for Beka and Derek, the Gluckman report and the new recommendations came out a few months too late. They'd spent thousands gutting a rental property of which the highest reading was 6.6 micrograms – well below the new safety levels. Speaking about it many years later, Derek tells me that to be honest he still feels a little sheepish about the whole thing, given he'd previously worked as a chemist testing residues of agrochemicals and already understood that the levels of meth they'd detected in their home were minuscule.

But he felt there was such a lack of information and science back then as to what the implications of those traces of meth were, and the void was so swiftly filled by meth-testing companies. Regardless of the findings of the Gluckman report, he feels they did what they had to do at the time. As for Beka, she just tries not to think about their meth-testing nightmare, it's simply too stressful. Her strategy for coping has been to block it out altogether.

In the aftermath, she originally started a Facebook support group with a friend for other homeowners who'd had their homes contaminated but eventually she found it all too tough. They did eventually re-tenant their Hamilton home, and when that tenant left they passed on doing a meth test.

She's still on the email distribution lists from some of the meth companies they dealt with throughout their ordeal and even long after the Gluckman report, some companies are still whipping up fear around meth. In July 2020, Meth Xpert's Simon Fleming was warning nearly $10 million of meth was being consumed in New Zealand properties every week – 'and not just any properties, but your investment properties, and possibly even the very family home you intend to purchase'. At Christmas time in another email to his client list that year he was advising them that they must test not only every room in their home for meth, but also every space, including wardrobes, linen cupboards and hot-water cupboards, to ensure their safety.

Even after a savaging from scientists and the government, meth testing companies are still sowing fear about contamination. Old habits die hard.

* * *

In late 2022, Housing Minister Megan Woods called a press conference in her office on the seventh floor of the Beehive to announce the government was seeking public feedback on Gluckman's proposed new limit of 15 micrograms of methamphetamine per 100cm^2 with an eye to making it law. In homes where meth has been cooked or just smoked, levels above 15 micrograms would be required to be cleaned up, and a landlord could be fined $4000 if they knowingly rent out a house above this level. That bizarre leap in logic, which had seen former meth labs treated the same as homes where the drug had only been smoked, was now being baked into legislation.

At 30 micrograms, a level at which it is believed manufacturing has occurred, a house would be deemed uninhabitable until the meth was cleaned up, while any possessions in the house would be deemed contaminated and be destroyed. There was evidence, Woods said, that people's health could be affected at 15 micrograms.

When I checked with Sir Peter Gluckman if that were true, his answer was succinct. 'No, absolutely not.'

So what does all of this mean? The dubious testing for infinitesimal traces of a drug that was once obtainable over the counter of your local pharmacy, and at vastly higher doses, looks set to stay.

People who insist on testing their homes for meth, may well end up spending tens of thousands of dollars decontaminating their homes if they're found to have a tiny trace of methamphetamine on a wall.

At the same press conference, HNZ, now Kāinga Ora, was granted an extension so it wasn't breaking the law for failing to comply with the timeframes set with the government's healthy homes standards. These require landlords to ensure their rental properties meet minimum standards around being warm and dry, important measures that ensure tenants live in homes free of things that are actually a risk to their health, like mould.

* * *

In early 2023 scientists from the University of Auckland revealed that their air pollution monitoring station on Customs Street near the bottom of Queen Street in the city had detected THC, caffeine, nicotine as well as tiny traces of methamphetamine in the air.

On average there were almost 25 picograms of meth per cubic metre of air – a picogram is one trillionth of a gram.

But you could breathe easy, the scientists reassured the public, it would take someone 8000 years of inhaling that air to get a single hit of P.

Like it or not, there are traces of meth all around us.

CHAPTER 7

DREAD PIRATE ROBERTS
Importing Drugs from the Dark Web

THESE DAYS, THE VAST MAJORITY OF METH THAT REACHES Aotearoa comes in through Tāmaki Makaurau, whether that be the airport, the port or the international mail centre – and not much stockpiling goes on. Detectives say that pretty much as soon as the meth gets in, it's on its way out, to be shortly smoked in a pipe. While there's no official estimate on how much meth is manufactured domestically at the moment, there are fewer meth labs being busted and the amount of precursor chemicals seized has fallen, too. One detective superintendent I spoke to said his best guess is home-cooked meth now accounts for only 20 per cent of the total, possibly less.

When police burst into former Warriors rugby league star and Kiwi international Manu Vatuvei's home in Papatoetoe in 2019, they found him and his brother Lopini Mafi opening the package of methamphetamine that had just been delivered to them by an undercover customs officer posing as a courier. The police also found digital scales, empty plastic bags used for selling meth and remnants of white powder, in multiple locations. On Lopini Mafi's phone, handily for the cops, were numerous videos and photos of the two of them joyfully opening previous packages of meth – that hadn't been intercepted.

Just months after winning television's *Dancing with the Stars* competition, Vatuvei was arrested and charged with importing and supplying methamphetamine. The brothers had used a contact in Africa to send the packages to New Zealand, which they would either consume themselves or supply to others. Vatuvei's lawyer told the court that the former footballer had found himself in a dark place after his marriage collapsed and injuries forced him to retire from professional sport. He'd turned to alcohol and drugs to try to cope with the fallout.

Vatuvei eventually pleaded guilty to one representative charge of importing 2 kilos of methamphetamine, and in March 2022 was sentenced to three and a half years in prison, while his brother, deemed the brains behind the unsophisticated operation, received a sentence of more than seven years. The judge told Vatuvei, who'd played 226 games for the Warriors and won the world cup with the Kiwi team in 2008, that his fall from grace was punishment in itself. 'Your final legacy in the community does not need to be defined by what happened today.'

The raid on his South Auckland home reflects the increasingly easy-to-access global supply chain, and a relatively new trend that police have started to notice: a lot more meth is getting shipped to Aotearoa from that continent, predominantly from South Africa. They suspect it's likely to be Afghan meth that's transported into Africa then shipped out across the Pacific. But whether the methamphetamine is getting cooked by cartels in the mountains of Mexico, by warlords in the badlands of Myanmar, by the super labs in Europe, or coming from Taliban-taxed meth makers in Afghanistan, some of it makes its way here.

That was the view of New Zealand's top drug cop, Blair Macdonald, the detective inspector who managed the country's National Drug Intelligence Bureau at the time of our interview in 2021. He has since left the force. The bureau is a multi-agency unit that includes the police, customs and health officials, and gathers strategic intelligence on illicit drugs and their precursors to try to get drugs off the streets. The results from Aotearoa's wastewater drug-testing also feeds into the bureau, allowing it to target law enforcement and support to certain locations. And it runs High Alert, an early warning system for potentially lethal illegal drugs whether they be tainted with dangerous substances like fentanyl, for example, or simply contain a dangerously strong dose.

For 15 years, Blair Macdonald worked on the police frontlines against drugs and organised crime, from conducting covert work to leading raids and literally kicking in the doors of suspected crooks. When we sat down to talk at the national headquarters in central Wellington, he told me the one clear trend regarding methamphetamine over his time in the force is the absolute proliferation of meth being imported into the country. Not only are records for the biggest busts at the border routinely broken but also run-of-the-mill seizures keep rising, and the testing of wastewater for P suggests meth is continuing to be consumed at pretty high levels. Even though domestic meth use decreased during the Covid pandemic because global shipping networks were disrupted, it didn't take long for it to bounce back, he said.

The combined Police and Customs seizure records illustrate his point. In 2014, New Zealand authorities seized 99 kilos of methamphetamine; 2015, it was 342 kilos, and in 2016 the amount almost tripled to nearly 950 kilos, thanks largely to the almost farcical attempts of a hare-brained group to land half a tonne of meth that had been deliberately dropped out at sea by a cargo ship just off the Far North's coast. Then, armed with neither local nor boating knowledge, the group's first attempt to collect the meth resulted in them getting the trailer of their heavy fibreglass boat stuck in the sand at Shipwreck Bay as they tried to launch it, drawing the attention of bemused locals who had to tow them out.

One of those who went to help was Ahipara builder Jeff Smith, who downed tools at the house he was building and went to take a look at what was going on. He later told local media that the group's attempt to launch their boat on this area of soft sandy beach – ideal for surfcasting – had been a comedy of errors. After a second attempt and successful launch, the group did manage to successfully collect the meth, but when they got back to shore they ran their boat aground on Te Oneroa-a-Tōhē/Ninety Mile Beach, ditched it there and took off, which again drew the attention of locals, who by this time had alerted the cops.

It didn't take long before the police pulled over some suspicious-looking folk in a campervan and searched the surrounding sand dunes. They seized 501 kilos, New Zealand's biggest bust at that time by a country mile, far eclipsing the 95-kilo shipment that had been seized at Auckland Airport a decade earlier. The police minister at the time of the bust,

Judith Collins, described it as wonderful and exciting. She was stoked that the Far North community had let their local cops know that this group 'looked a bit funny'. Builder Jeff Smith reckoned they would have got away with it scot-free had they not just abandoned their boat on the beach. 'It was unbelievable, it was the biggest news here in forever,' he told a reporter.

The amount of meth seized declined for the next several years: 477 kilos in 2017, 280 kilos in 2018, before shattering the records again in 2019 with 1846 kilos of crystal meth seized. A massive bust in September that year at the Ports of Auckland uncovered 469 kilos of meth hidden inside 60 electric motors. It had arrived in a shipping container that had left Thailand and was searched because Customs suspected it could have links to an overseas criminal syndicate, thought to be The Company/Sam Gor. It was estimated that that much meth could supply Aotearoa for more than half a year. In connecting raids carried out at properties across Auckland following the seizure, another 26 kilos of meth were found and police successfully prosecuted two Canadian nationals and one Aucklander for the importation. When sentencing them, Justice Toogood described the almost half-tonne haul as a 'virtual mountain of misery'.

It also meant the port authorities could save face, as just a few months earlier, another container at the port which was suspected of being jam-packed full of meth was whisked off the docks on the back of a truck before Customs could search it – with the help of an inside man, or in this case, woman. Officially, the container was full of air compressors from Thailand, but given that the company that imported it had recently been set up by a member of the Mongols Motorcycle Club, who had been freshly deported from Australia, Customs had decided it might be prudent to take a look inside. By the time the container was eventually found, it was empty, while the Ports of Auckland supervisor who used her security clearance to arrange for the container's hasty departure was found with $90,000 cash in a shoebox.

In August 2019, two British men were arrested after police found 200 kilos of meth in a wardrobe in a central Auckland apartment, this stash again linked to an overseas syndicate. It turned out that was a very busy week for the police in Auckland because residents out walking at Te Henga/Bethells Beach on Auckland's west coast had just stumbled upon $3 million worth of cocaine washed up on the shore. It is believed it had been dumped at sea off the New South Wales coast by drug smugglers a year earlier when their rigid inflatable boat was spotted by the Australian Border Force.

After 2019's bumper year of meth interceptions, the following year Covid-19 took hold, and the worldwide outbreaks and lockdowns affected global shipping routes and just 300 kilos of meth was seized in New Zealand in 2020. The virus affected the meth market in other ways too. Detective Inspector Macdonald said not only did the purity of meth noticeably decline, but in the South Island, wastewater testing showed consumption of meth had pretty much dried up within about a week of the country moving into Level 4 lockdown in March 2020. There was no way to distribute it around the country and the greatly reduced supply led to a big jump in prices on the street in Auckland. A gram had been going for as little as $200 pre-Covid in the city; it didn't take long for that price to double. As our borders reopened, pretty soon normal services resumed. In March 2022, Customs and police made a new record bust at Auckland International Airport – 613 kilos of methamphetamine, with a street value the police estimated to be $245 million. That record didn't stand for long.

In early 2023, police arrested five men in rural Helensville who were believed to be involved in a shipment of 713 kilos of meth concealed in bottles of maple syrup shipped from Canada.

One recent police report suggested there may be around 300 clan labs operating in New Zealand but of various pedigree, and they acknowledge it is simply so much cheaper now to import meth from abroad than to cook it here. And part of the problem for police is that this country is such a highly valuable market to export meth to. Blair Macdonald said New Zealand sits in the top three countries in the world in terms of the domestic price of meth, just below Hong Kong but above Australia. With limited resources, and around a million shipping containers arriving in the country a year, the amount of meth that is actually being stopped probably isn't very high at all, he admits.

A few years ago, I talked to a source who has intimate knowledge of the various ways methamphetamine gets into the country, and one common ploy of Asian crime groups is to mislead the police with an informant. The supposed rat passes intelligence to the cops about a shipment of meth arriving here, and while this is true, a much bigger amount is arriving elsewhere, simultaneously sacrificing one delivery and diverting the authorities' attention. So, while the police might be putting out press releases celebrating a big meth bust, the receivers are celebrating too; everybody's happy.

The high price that methamphetamine can fetch in New Zealand is one of the reasons the United States Drug Enforcement Administration (DEA) posted an agent to its Wellington embassy in late 2020, with more staff expected to follow. In an interview with the news outlet Re:, DEA attaché Brian Fleming said he's spent several decades working on cases involving Colombian cocaine traffickers and the activities of Mexican cartels. Now he's been assigned to help solidify the DEA's working relationship with the NZ Police to ensure more information is shared. The goal is to disrupt the international drug syndicates, which he warned will exploit any market where there's money to be made. And there's phenomenal money to be made by getting drugs into New Zealand. For example, Fleming said in the United States a kilo of meth costs about NZ$7000, it's much cheaper again in Mexico – but by the time it gets to Aotearoa, that kilo of meth is worth 20 times as much.

But it's not all cartels and huge quantities of meth being hidden inside shipping containers. The police are finding that more and more New Zealanders, without any connections to the international or domestic gangs or dealers, are getting high-quality methamphetamine delivered right to their front door, simply by ordering it over the internet on the dark web. What's more, if your meth package is intercepted, many companies promise to ship again, and again, until it gets through – delivery guaranteed.

Detective Inspector Macdonald told me it first really dawned on him what the authorities are up against when he stood on the floor of the New Zealand Post International Mail Centre in Auckland, with its conveyor belts filled with all kinds of mail, running 24 hours a day. And with the methods of concealing P only limited by people's imaginations, finding the parcels with meth in them is like finding a needle in a haystack. Therefore, even if one or two packages are intercepted, the odds are that many others will get through.

Yet obviously it tends to be the packages that don't get through that become public knowledge. In December 2013, 23-year-old Dylan Richardson stood in the dock of Palmerston North District Court on charges of importing and supplying $15,000 worth of methamphetamine after Customs intercepted a package with 15 grams of P that he'd bought on the infamous 'Silk Road' website. When authorities searched his home, they found another gram of the drug, plus ziplock bags for divvying it up to sell and a grand total of $440 in cash. Pablo Escobar he was not. His lawyer told the court Richardson had turned to methamphetamine during a period of personal upheaval in his life, his sister had recently died and his father had suffered a stroke just days after her funeral. Nevertheless, he was sentenced to two years and four months in jail, the judge telling him he was confident he would be released at the first opportunity.

* * *

Just two months prior, and at the opposite end of the narcotics chain, another young man was being closely surveilled by a team of FBI agents as he worked on his laptop while sitting in the science fiction section of a San Francisco public library. The team of agents were exercising extreme caution so as not to spook him, because the success of the operation hinged not so much on physically capturing him but ensuring he wasn't able to close the lid of his heavily encrypted laptop before they nabbed him. The FBI believed that the 29-year-old Ross Ulbricht, using the public wifi in the library that October day, was better known as Dread Pirate Roberts (his online persona based on a character from *The Princess Bride*) and the creator of the Silk Road website. Ulbricht was literally making millions by facilitating online drug sales; a modern-day digital drug lord. Silk Road is invisible to traditional internet searches, being on the dark web, and since launching just a couple of years earlier it had already hosted tens of thousands of sales of illicit drugs. Marijuana and cocaine were site favourites, but methamphetamine was also easy to come by as were prescription medications, fake IDs and at times even firearms. As one American journalist described it: 'Silk Road was Amazon with a black-market bent.'

Dread Pirate Roberts gave an interview to *Forbes* in August 2013 in which he said that the idea behind Silk Road was to pair the TOR browser, which protects users' privacy by masking their location and identity, with the crypto-currency Bitcoin, to create an anonymous marketplace. He added that he'd taken over running Silk Road from the original Dread Pirate Roberts. In that interview he was asked if he felt any moral guilt about selling highly addictive and dangerous drugs.

'On the contrary,' he responded, 'I am proud of what I am doing. I can't think of one drug that doesn't have at least some harmful effects. That's really not the point, though. People own themselves, they own their own bodies, and it is their right to put into their bodies whatever they choose. Giving people that freedom of choice, the dignity of self-ownership, is a good thing.'

Drug users should be held accountable if they hurt people, he argued but criminalising drug users and throwing them in cages causes communities more harm 'than drugs ever could'.

It was the open defiance of such US laws that had seen the capture of Dread Pirate Roberts become a top priority for the FBI, Homeland Security, the Drug Enforcement Administration and the Internal Revenue Service. And as Ulbricht sat in the window seat of the San Francisco library that day, he was unwittingly chatting online to an undercover federal agent who had infiltrated the operation and was working as a Silk Road employee, and who was asking Ulbricht at that very moment to log in and fix a technical issue on the website.

Just as he did so, two plainclothes FBI agents were given the green light to move in and carry out the sting. The male and female agents approached Ulbricht, starting a rowdy argument with one another, the dispute momentarily distracting Ulbricht and allowing one of the agents to swiftly slide the laptop off the desk, still opened, the other placing a stunned Ulbricht under arrest.

An FBI digital forensics expert was quickly handed the laptop and established that it had access to Silk Road's server, financial records and the mastermind page usually only accessible to Dread Pirate Roberts. The FBI were sure they had their man. Following the arrest, the FBI announced that it had shut down the most sophisticated and extensive criminal marketplace on the internet. It stated that Silk Road turned over a billion dollars' worth of sales in just two years. Ulbricht's former girlfriend, Julia Vie, said while she knew he had been up to something shady, she had no idea how big the operation was, but that he never spent any of the money he'd made.

'He may have been book smart,' she told a reporter following his arrest, 'but he definitely wasn't street smart. He was not at all a drug kingpin ... I mean most kingpins buy furs and jewels and they're living the life. Ross didn't even have a car.'

In May 2015 in a Manhattan federal court, Ulbricht was given two life sentences plus 40 years without parole for good measure for operating Silk Road. Prosecutors said he had personally made around $18 million in commissions on drug sales, and during sentencing the judge was particularly critical of his attempts to have hitmen murder five individuals Ulbricht believed posed a threat. It was questionable of the judge to mention the five attempted hits, given Ulbricht was never charged over these, nevertheless, when he shuffled out of the courtroom in chains that day, Ross Ulbricht carried the photos of five people who had overdosed and died after consuming drugs they'd bought on Silk Road.

October 2022 marked the start of Ulbricht's tenth year in a high-security prison in Tucson, Arizona, the government having thrown him in the cage he'd raged against. He now spends his days acting as a mediator on his wing, made up of other non-violent drug offenders, and he's frequently put on watch to support other prisoners who want to kill themselves. His mother runs a website, freeross.org, where she argues how he is a very young, peaceful yet misguided entrepreneur and that the judge had been unduly swayed by the unproven and unprosecuted allegations about the hitmen before delivering such a draconian sentence. Around half a million people have signed a petition to free him. In addition to selling a range of 'Free Ross' hoodies, caps and shirts, freeross.org features quotes from a host of prominent Americans such as Noam Chomsky, who says his sentence was far too harsh for a first-time non-violent offender and was a shocking miscarriage of justice.

Yet, within weeks of Dread Pirate Roberts' arrest in 2013, a new site was up and running under the same name and with an identical look; Silk Road 2.0 was born. And the new operator of the site, still going by the moniker Dread Pirate Roberts, told a digital reporter from the news site *Mashable* that when he was inevitably caught, there would be someone ready to take his place. 'You can take down the man but you can't take down the idea.' Just half a year later, Silk Road 2.0 followed the fate of its predecessor and was busted by authorities and its administrators appeared before the courts. As they tried the case, Manhattan attorney Preet Bharara delivered the following message: 'Let's be clear. This Silk Road, in whatever form, is the road to prison.'

The United Nations' Office on Drugs and Crime recently commissioned a report into drug sales on the dark web and while it found that sales were tiny compared to the overall illicit drug market – well under one per cent – it found the number of people buying drugs online has exploded in recent years and the drugs available vary from region to region. It estimates dark-web drug sales were worth about $80 million around

2011; by 2020 it was well over $300 million. One survey of drug users across 50 countries found the proportion of those who had bought drugs over the dark web had more than tripled from under 5 per cent in 2014 to 15 per cent in 2020.

* * *

One evening, with a more technologically minded mate than me, we surfed the dark web to see what was on offer for people interested in bringing drugs illegally into New Zealand. Some sites specialised in cut-price black-market pharmaceuticals like Viagra, Xanax, tramadol and oxycodone. Others offered an array of illicit substances for sale from Afghan heroin to Colombian or Peruvian cocaine, ketamine, LSD and plenty of designer chemicals promising psychedelic experiences. There was also a plethora of options for those interested in importing crystal meth: one site offered 5 grams of crystal methamphetamine for NZ$200, 10 grams for $320; another was offering 50 grams for around $1300.

With prices ranging from $26–$40 for a gram of crystal meth on the dark web, a gram at that time was retailing in Wellington at around $500, illustrating the potentially huge return on investment for people willing to take the risk and on-sell the drugs if they get through. But while these sites appear to have a smorgasbord of drugs available, it's user-beware – finding a reputable seller isn't always easy and that's because many of the dark web sites are, or eventually become, scams. The average life expectancy of such sites is just eight months, according to the United Nations Office on Drugs and Crime, which found that most of them selling drugs in 2019 had only been launched the previous year, and in addition to raids by authorities, the sites often employ hackers to prey upon one another. It's the wild west of the internet.

In 2017, Auckland police executed Operation Tiger, which was aimed at affluent teenagers across the city who had been repeatedly importing drugs over the dark web, often ordering them from the comfort of their parents' living rooms. Some of them were still at school while others had recently left. The police made 13 arrests and laid 79 charges, seizing an array of MDMA, meth, speed, LSD, cocaine and cannabis. The officer in charge of the raids, Detective Sergeant Tim Williams, said the unusual thing about Operation Tiger was that most of the young adults they arrested had never had any prior dealings with the police at all. These kids weren't hardened criminals, or even particularly street smart, often mailing the drugs to their own homes, but they were able to easily navigate the dark web and order large amounts of drugs online.

Once the drugs are in the country, social media platforms like Facebook, Instagram and Snapchat are brilliant at connecting dealers with new customers. I know a guy who found someone advertising meth for sale in Auckland on a closed Facebook page, and after others on the site vouched that he was legit, he bought 2 grams of meth and had it personally delivered to him before a Warriors game at Mt Smart Stadium – not by Manu Vatuvei.

In Dunedin, young mum Tamra Smith found herself standing before a judge after the police cottoned on to the mobile drug business she was running via Snapchat. Her profile gave some clue: 'budzindudz 2.0', where she advertised an array of drugs including cannabis, ecstasy and LSD, even delivering them around the city. After watching Smith post that she would be out and about selling 'a gram at $250, skunk fids ($50 cannabis bag) and $30 LSD jubes', an undercover police officer named Lee arranged to buy three jubes from her for $90 and met her outside a local restaurant, did the deal, and then swiftly brought her budding enterprise to a halt. Sentencing her to nine months home detention in 2020, the judge told Smith, 'The police are on social media networks. The police can catch you out and, in your case, did catch you out.'

In the United States, the Drug Enforcement Administration has even released an 'emoji drug code' document aimed at helping parents and educators understand the coded emojis that are used in conjunction with illegal drugs, the DEA warning that drugs like meth and fentanyl are widely available on social media and that anyone with a smartphone can buy them.

> Drug dealer advertising: 👜 💰 💵 🚀 💨
> High potency: 🚀 🍫 💥
> Big batch: 🍪
> Universal for drugs: 🍁
> Meth: 💉 💎 ❤️ 🧊
> Marijuana: 🍃 🌴 🔥 💥 😵 🍀 ☘️
> Magic Mushrooms: 🍄
> Adderall: 💊

One the questions Blair Macdonald gets asked again and again by police officers who are making the busts and taking down meth dealers around Aotearoa is whether these arrests and seizures have any impact on the overall meth market, and unfortunately, he tells them, the ESR wastewater results show the answer is always no. Because, while you might take out a drug dealer in a small town or intercept a particular shipment, you're not doing anything to deter demand for the drug, and drug users are incredibly resourceful people by nature, so they'll simply find another source to buy from.

In a statement that might have been unthinkable not long ago from a senior police officer, Macdonald told me there's just no way New Zealand can arrest itself out of its meth problem. That's not to say the police haven't given it their best shot: the number of people arrested for possessing P tripled between 2010 and 2020. To be fair, in the last couple of years, meth users, particularly young ones, have been increasingly referred to health and addiction services instead of being prosecuted and it's a policy Macdonald fully supports because he says that until addiction is addressed, we'll never get on top of the P problem. This is something we'll be exploring soon.

For so many people who are addicted to meth, it's an opportunity to escape a hopeless situation, even if it's just for an hour or two. After 20 years investigating and battling the meth trade, Macdonald believes meth is often over-hyped, that P can clearly cause a lot of harm but there are plenty who will use P and who are perfectly capable of picking a glass pipe up and putting it down again, too. At the time of our interview, he was also confident that overall meth use was naturally declining. Wastewater testing carried out by the Institute of Environmental Science and Research (ESR) suggested meth use had fallen over the previous few years, with estimates of a decrease from about 14 kilos a week to around 12.

Macdonald believes Covid-19 may have played a part but he also feels many people now view P as a 'junkie drug', one that's capable of destroying your life and the lives of your whānau, and that people are switching to a different drug – because the amount of MDMA being detected in our wastewater is soaring. MDMA, or ecstasy, he said, is a much more socially acceptable drug, with everyone from teenagers to those in their 40s and 50s willing to partake. Offering someone a line of MDMA at a house party is probably going to go down a lot better than pulling out a glass pipe to smoke meth.

But by mid-2022, the amount of meth being detected in our wastewater began rising again. A senior scientist at ESR, Andrew Chappell, told me they were now regularly detecting 17 to 18 kilos of methamphetamine a week, and they'd recently had one week where they had hit a record 20 kilograms – a level of consumption up more than a third on the year before. And while they can't tell if that means there are lots more people using or whether it's the same number using much more, it seems New Zealand's appetite for P remains undiminished.

* * *

In Prague a group of scientists have raised fears that the methamphetamine users could unwittingly be turning fish into addicts as a result of P in their pee and poo. Some behavioural ecologists at a Czech University recreated in the lab the levels of meth contamination found in rivers downstream from wastewater plants in Europe. They put 60 brown trout in a tank with water laced with one microgram of meth per litre, for two months.

When the trout were eventually removed from the tank, they moved around a lot less than the meth-free trout in the control group. The trout with the most meth in their brain tissue moved the least, leading the researchers to conclude the trout were addicted and going into withdrawal.

The trout from both the meth tank and control tank were also given the choice to swim in two different streams of water, one with meth and one without, and those fish who had been in the meth tank chose to swim in the meth-laced water.

In its coverage of the findings in an article titled 'Trout can become addicted to meth. Here's why that's so scary', *National Geographic* warned that with brown trout being an important source of food for many predators, any change in their behaviour could reverberate up the food chain. It also interviewed a behavioural neuroscientist who said that when fish become dependent on drugs they can choose to spend more time near wastewater pipes or run-off, to keep getting their hit, rather than moving about and spreading nutrients more evenly throughout the environment. P-fiend fish could disrupt the ecology of rivers.

CHAPTER 8
WHITE-COLLAR 'CHEMICAL MAN'
Professionals Run Ragged

> We have a bright technological future with chemicals but only if we resolve in our minds how to handle the problems posed by the small percentage of people who cannot handle the use of drugs.
>
> Ray Henwood, 'Living with Drugs'

AT THE BOTTOM OF THE GOVERNMENT'S REPORT INTO DRUG abuse and dependency in 1973 was an essay penned by Ray Henwood from Victoria University, Wellington, titled 'Living with Drugs'. Since man's earliest days as a social animal, he wrote, we have turned to plants and roots that not only provide relief when experiencing pain but also others that allow periods of euphoria, hallucination and intoxication, to escape briefly from the boredom and repetition of everyday existence.

Yet with the more recent development of drugs like aspirin, Benzedrine, codeine and morphine, we were no longer dependent upon the natural environment directly for our drugs but could now extract or tailor-make chemicals for specific medical or recreational purposes.

New Zealand needed to face up to the fact that the age of the 'chemical man' had dawned. But the real question was not why do people use drugs, we always have and always will, he said, but why do some people become addicted to or mastered by drugs while the vast majority of users escape such a fate?

And while it was always popular to blame the substance itself, in the case of alcohol the 'demon drink', Henwood wrote society was slowly realising that poor social conditions can lead to major misuse of a drug in society.

It was time to stop law enforcement shouldering so much of the burden and devise a system where drugs are used and controlled in the best possible way, while those who can't handle them are given treatment and support.

* * *

As he sat in the TV3 news studio and the countdown to the six o'clock bulletin was underway, the presenter Darren McDonald was dealing with a rather peculiar problem. The words he was preparing to read were jumping off the autocue and dancing around the room, which is not ideal when you're about to deliver New Zealanders their prime-time news. It was only moments before they went live that McDonald used all his focus and concentration to put the words back into order, pull them back onto the autocue and begin to read the news.

What the public and his colleagues didn't realise was that McDonald was as high as a kite on methamphetamine. And this wasn't just a one-off; there were many times in the early 2000s when he was beamed into Kiwi living rooms, while

Mum, Dad and the kids were eating dinner, and he was rocked by P.

And the more he did it, the more of a thrill it became. 'It was simply exhilarating,' McDonald told a reporter a few years later, 'to do drugs and then read the news bulletin. It was so much fun to be doing something so secret so publicly.'

Originally from Queensland, Darren McDonald's first experience with drugs was when he took an ecstasy pill at Sydney's Gay and Lesbian Mardi Gras when he was 21 years old. He absolutely loved it – and then as a TV newsreader in Australia, his celebrity status became the ticket he needed to gain entry to Sydney's biggest shows, even partying with stars like Billy Idol and Eddie Murphy. As TVNZ's *Sunday* put it, his life in Sydney had become one of A-list stars and A-class drugs, and cocaine was the drug of choice. McDonald admits he got totally caught up in the fun that was there to be had, and that cocaine and ecstasy helped break down his social barriers, boost his stunted self-confidence and helped him become his best gay self. He was free to party and free to dance.

When he moved to New Zealand in the late 1990s and began presenting the weekend news with TV3, someone offered him a hit from a P pipe and he didn't hesitate. The next day he was buying a point of meth, or a tenth of a gram, for $100.

As his appetite for P grew, he began spending $1000 a week on the drug, which left him in constant debt. The seemingly successful newsreader in the limelight at night was having his car repossessed come daylight. By the early 2000s, he was also regularly getting into trouble. He was beaten up in an Auckland waterfront bar. In early 2001 he was caught drink-driving in

Ponsonby, his lawyer telling the court McDonald had simply misjudged the amount he'd drunk because he hadn't had a meal – he was nearly double the alcohol limit.

As well as an increase in overall meth users at around this time in New Zealand was an alarming number of professionals, such as McDonald, trying to keep up appearances but running themselves ragged on meth. In about 2003, a blogger Russell Brown wrote that 'middle-class P users know they will never go on to shoot someone during a robbery, but what they are risking is becoming embarrassing idiots with no money, and with other idiots for friends.'

Things really came crashing down for McDonald in late 2002. The police had bugged the premises of his meth dealer the year before, a penthouse suite at Auckland's Duxton Hotel, and on one of McDonald's regular visits there, he was observed offering to sell his dealer nine ecstasy tablets that a mate of his had brought into the country. The police subsequently raided McDonald's home, he was arrested and charged, TV3 promptly suspended him and he quit the job not long after.

Initially, McDonald protested his innocence and vowed to fight the 'scurrilous' charges against him. He was adamant that once his case got to trial, the truth would be heard and he would be cleared of them. But shortly before his High Court trial, in 2003, he pleaded guilty to two charges relating to the supply of ecstasy and methamphetamine and ended up receiving a rather lenient sentence of eight months' home detention. It was his former job that saved him from a stint in prison, the judge saying that his celebrity status would make a custodial sentence unduly harsh. Justice Marion Frater told him that the involvement of high profile, intelligent people like himself in the drug trade 'gives the erroneous impression that drug use is OK. It's not.'

Outside the court, a television reporter summed up the case as 'a tragic story of addiction, of a man who appeared to have it all but lost everything because of his dependence on methamphetamine'. Darren McDonald, looking clearly relieved that he wasn't heading for Mount Eden prison, delivered a message to those watching his fate unfold on the nightly news bulletin he used to present: 'I have a great many regrets,' he said. 'Just don't do drugs, everyone.'

Asked what he was going to do for the rest of the day, he said he was going home to have a drink.

The media in both New Zealand and Australia dined out on the case of the fallen prime-time presenter; the *Woman's Day* magazine ran the story 'TV3's disgraced newsreader'; another headline stated: 'I read the news high on drugs'; and a weekend newspaper summed it up as 'Star's drug shame'. After the dust had settled, McDonald described being busted as the best thing that ever happened to him because he stopped using meth straight away and he hadn't disgraced himself, he argued, he'd discovered himself.

The same year Darren McDonald was convicted, it was estimated that between 2 and 3 per cent of adults in New Zealand had used amphetamines within the last 12 months, that included both speed and P. Other stats surfaced as well. Around 7 per cent of us had taken amphetamines at some point in our lives, and men were significantly more likely to do so than women – 9 per cent to 5 per cent respectively.

An Auckland rehab centre, Higher Ground, reported that the number of people it was treating for meth dependency had tripled, while the average age of those it was helping had dropped from 35 to 21 years. The Auckland City Mission had also noticed a jump in meth users accessing its detox centre, while treatment agencies in South Auckland, the Bay of Plenty and the East Cape reported similar trends.

The police were already run off their feet responding to the explosion in the number of meth labs, and occasionally explosions in them. They averaged one or two lab busts a year in the mid-to-late 1990s; in 2003 alone, they raided just over 200 labs, and recipes for cooking methamphetamine were now easily accessible on the internet.

The surge in meth had virtually come out of nowhere, all of a sudden a lot more of us were picking up a glass pipe. In 1998, when Kiwi adults were asked which drugs they'd used over the past 12 months in a national drug survey, just 0.1 per cent said they'd used crystal meth. By 2001, 0.9 per cent said they'd tried P in the past year.

Meth was becoming much more mainstream.

* * *

Over a few pints at an Auckland pub in 2021 I chatted with an early adopter, for anonymity's sake let's call him Steve, who told me all about his experience with P.

The first time he tried meth was in his west Auckland flat. It was 1999. His mate had bought a point, which came as a yellowy-brownish paste, and together they broke a lightbulb and used it as a pipe to smoke their first hit. It led to a fucking great night partying and dancing at Bed Bar on Auckland's Karangahape Road, talking nonsense with mates and feeling like he was floating, until the festivities wound up and he called it a night at around 5 am.

For many years afterwards, meth was never really a problem for Steve, he could buy a point for $100 and have a smoke and leave the rest in his bedside drawer for a month or two or until the next time he went clubbing with his mates; or he'd use it as a nice little pick-me-up in the morning after a night out taking ecstasy. He went on his big OE and didn't touch meth for years, but when he returned he continued to flirt with the drug. Then about four or five years ago, now a qualified school teacher, he began using more and more. He'd met a new mate who had good connections for buying meth, the occasional weekend imbibing with others eventually became weekday use, until soon, Steve was regularly smoking by himself.

Watching the meth start to smoke in the pipe was the coolest part, he reckoned, admiring the way the crystals would burn and the white smoke would swirl in the glass pipe before he inhaled. It became his little ritual.

And then one Monday, after a big weekend, Steve had a few puffs before he went to school in the morning to help get him through the day. Bad idea. He spent the day paranoid as hell, trying to avoid eye contact with his colleagues, constantly checking the state of his eyes with his cellphone and in the bathroom, but he was pretty sure no one knew. After getting over that first day at work on meth jitters, Steve started taking his pipe with him into the bathroom at home when he showered in the mornings to start the day high.

He had several main contacts he'd use to get meth, one he'd meet out the back of a Mangere tavern and hand over his money. The contact would hop into a car across the carpark with a member of the Head Hunters and come back and deliver his P. But one day his contact turned up with a pair of black eyes and from then they bought their meth from a Mongrel Mob pad in Mangere, with bullet holes in the door.

Of course, buying meth doesn't always go smoothly. One time a trusted dealer just walked off with $2000 cash and wasn't seen again for weeks. Steve could also get meth from another mate who was closely connected to a syndicate that brought serious quantities of methamphetamine and synthetic analogues into the country. On two occasions this guy had a kilo of methamphetamine stolen from him: once betrayed by an associate, the other time when a drug deal was going down in a carpark and a Nissan Skyline raced in. Clearly having been tipped off about the deal, a patched gang member emerged from the car wielding a shotgun and made off with his kilo of meth. The financial impact of having no drugs to sell, after spending several hundred thousand dollars on two kilos of meth, delivered a fatal blow to his business and Steve didn't hear from his mate anymore.

But more frequently, when buys went bad it was because the meth was shit, and he'd realise as soon as he put it in the pipe; the P would burn black, not white, and it wouldn't have any real effect. He noticed a big difference in the quality of meth as a result of the pandemic too. With global shipping in turmoil, the usual crystal meth he'd buy just wasn't around, instead dealers were hawking 'old school' meth – just like the yellowy paste he'd tried back in 1999.

When supplies started getting through, however, Steve was being offered what dealers assured him was high-quality Mexican crystal meth for $700 a gram. This was steep. Before Covid, Steve could buy a quarter ounce – seven grams – for $250 a gram.

During New Zealand's first lockdown in 2020, Steve's meth use rapidly escalated. With no work to go to, he spent his days smoking heavily and gambling online, winning and then promptly losing large sums of money. Then lockdown was over and it was time to go back to school. And while at first a few puffs would get him through the day, soon he needed more – soon he was smoking P in the toilets, popping out at lunchtime to smoke in fast-food restaurant bathrooms, smoking on school camps, and smoking on the way to and from school.

But it wasn't enjoyable anymore. Now it was just to get by, because he knew when he stopped he'd just fucking crash. This wasn't fun, it was pure survival.

He felt bad doing it at school and near the kids but it never stopped him. At the time he thought he was still teaching to a high level but in hindsight he realises he was making mistakes, he looked dishevelled and felt constantly flat. He'd find any excuse to smoke – to get through a meeting, to celebrate the meeting ending. The more meth he did, the more antisocial he became, cutting back on contact with his mates and when he did catch up with them he'd get bored and make excuses to leave. He'd just hang out with people who were also sitting around smoking meth – the kind of people you wouldn't want anyone to know that you knew.

He was running low on money, his credit cards were maxed out and one day he consumed a gram in a day, which is a lot of meth to be using and a lot of money to be spending when you're not having fun.

He dabbled in a little dealing himself and bought scales. One of the oddities of the meth market, he told me, is that while the price of P may have collapsed to $250–300 a gram, many street dealers still sell a point of meth for $100; the same price they charged when a gram cost $1000. As we sat chopping a jug of Tiger beer at the Zookeeper's Son in Mt Roskill on that Friday afternoon, Steve told me he had used P for 161 days in a row in 2020. He was buying and consuming an eight-ball (3.5 grams) a week and spending between $900 and $1200 a week on meth.

Eventually Steve called a counsellor through the free service available through schools and talked about his troubles, even having a hit of P during their conversation, which he found amusing. But while he might have been high, what the counsellor talked to him about registered – his gambling, the death of a parent, and how Steve was the only person who had the power to change things. It helped put things in perspective and Steve set Easter 2021 as his quit date. Just before, he drove up the road and smoked everything he had left, then went home and filmed himself smashing his pipe to pieces, and he biffed all his lighters, bag and broken pipe in the rubbish.

He'd tried quitting a few times before, but never really meant it, but he noticed that it didn't matter if he'd binged for a week or 161 days: coming off it was identical. He spent the next three or four days exhausted, sleeping and feeling down and moping around, and then he came right. That was three months ago. Since then he said he's put on about 12 kilos, he's sleeping better, eating well and generally just a whole lot happier.

But what surprised me as we finished our beers and wrapped up our interview, given what I'd just heard over the last couple of hours about meth and its addictiveness, and seeing this from a professional's perspective, was that Steve still said he doesn't think meth's really that bad. He said he's never missed a bill, he's never stolen anything or got into a fight, and apart from using meth, he hasn't committed any crime, he hasn't harmed anyone – well, except for himself.

Steve and Darren McDonald are just a couple of the countless people in New Zealand whose financial, professional and personal lives have been turned upside down because they've been unable to put down the pipe.

* * *

When it comes to getting a handle on just how many of us within New Zealand are using methamphetamine, and other illegal substances for that matter, the most comprehensive look into drug use came when the Ministry of Health carried out a drug-use survey in 2007–2008. Nearly 6800 New Zealanders were asked whether they'd taken illicit drugs for recreational purposes, which drugs they'd used, how often they took them, whether they took risks while high and if they'd ever experienced problems or tried to seek help in terms of stopping using.

Extrapolating those results, pretty much half of us have used illicit drugs for recreational purposes at some point in our lives, and unsurprisingly, cannabis is the clear winner. In the land of the long white cloud, 46 per cent said they'd smoked pot, 6 per cent of adults had tried ecstasy, 7 per cent LSD, and just over 7 per cent had tried amphetamines. Two per cent of adults, around 55,000 people, had used amphetamines in the previous 12 months, with around half saying they'd had meth, the other half, speed. (And while the survey distinguished between meth and speed, it also noted that, in Aotearoa, speed often doesn't contain amphetamine sulphate and often what people think is speed is actually powdered meth.)

The survey suggested most people who use meth take it very infrequently. While half of those who had taken amphetamines reported only doing so once or twice in the past 12 months, a quarter had used it at least monthly, while one in seven were using weekly. It found that men were twice as likely as women to have used amphetamines, those aged 18–24 were using in the greatest numbers, while Māori and Europeans were more likely to be using than Pasifika and Asians. One in three amphetamine users had driven a vehicle while high and lots had been to work while under the influence too.

Since that survey was carried out 15 years ago, an annual New Zealand Health Survey has been taken, where people are asked about their drug use in the past year. Pretty consistently, around one per cent of respondents now say they've tried meth – remember that's down from around 3 per cent in 2003.

In 2019–2020, that equated to 45,000 Kiwis having used meth in the previous 12 months. It's likely to be an underestimate, though, as those in prison are excluded from the survey and are a heavy drug-using group, judging from a 2015 Corrections commissioned report that showed half of all inmates who were either on remand or freshly sentenced had used meth at some point while out in the community, many of them recently. But most people who use meth will do so infrequently and the Drug Foundation has calculated that there's probably between 6000 and 8000 people responsible for the bulk of P consumption in this country.

And another stat – when it comes to meth use in New Zealand, it's also a tale of two islands. Not only do the police intercept far fewer consignments of meth in, and heading for, the South Island but also their wastewater testing consistently shows it is MDMA that is the most widely used drug on the mainland, not meth. (Wastewater testing can't accurately detect cannabis levels – so it's not included). People also have to pay a lot more for P in the South Island. When the median price for a gram of meth in many North Island towns was $450 a few years back, in the south it was selling for $650.

In 2021, *The New Zealand Herald* analysed the wastewater testing results across the country in order to identify which towns used the most meth per person, and there were no South Island towns in the top 10 and only one in the top 20 – Westport snuck in at fifteenth. Apparently, they were getting through 5.69 grams of P per 1000 people each week in Westport. Kaitāia took out first place by a mile. They were said to be consuming well over 14 grams of P per 1000 people every week, but a police source said more testing was needed before it could officially be crowned New Zealand's meth capital. The top six – Kaitāia, Ōpōtiki, Wairoa, Kawerau, Tokoroa and Huntly – are all in the central or upper North Island and are all economically deprived towns.

* * *

Two years after the 'chemical man' essay was published, researchers at the University of Otago began a long-running project, called the Christchurch Health and Development Study, that has recently begun to shed some light not only on Henwood's questions but also wider psychosocial reasons for why only some people become addicted to drugs while the vast majority who try them do not. In 1977, the university began tracking the health, education and life progress of 1265 babies who were born in Canterbury between April and August that year. For the first few years, the researchers interviewed the children's mothers and then their teachers when they started school, and when the children turned seven, they were interviewed by the researchers too – all sorts of questions about their behaviour, their friends, their health and development, and so on.

As the children hit their teens, they were asked when they first drank alcohol and about the first time they got drunk; their answers used to inform research about whether these could be predictors of substance use later in life. They were quizzed about when they first had a puff of a cigarette, and whether they'd ever tried cannabis: at age 13, five of the kids had tried cannabis. By 18 years old, half of them had. When the group reached adulthood, whether they'd ever used methamphetamine was one of the topics they were surveyed about.

In 2020 they published their findings, with this headline-grabbing statement: 'Almost a third of middle-aged New Zealanders have tried methamphetamine at least once.' Their press release revealed a whopping 28 per cent of those in the study had used meth at least once between the ages of 18 and 35. It turns out people born in the late 1970s really like drinking and drugs, the study's director Professor Joe Boden told me over a Zoom call. Most of the participants who'd tried meth had only done so once or twice, others a little more frequently but were never regular users, then there were the 51 people (4 per cent) who had gone on to use P multiple times a week at some point in their lives.

Boden explained that the researchers were interested in trying to figure out the overall rate of meth use but also, what the predictors of meth use are, and which factors might influence whether someone simply dabbled with meth or became a heavy user.

And one of the key factors involved in whether someone is likely to experiment with meth in the first place, or any drugs for that matter, is personality. It turns out, having a strong tendency towards the trait known as 'novelty seeking', connected to an openness to experience, makes people way more likely to try drugs. Those who find they quite like getting high are likely to keep on wanting to get high, Boden said. This may explain the likes of Steve or Darren McDonald and others who are or were in the heavy-user category.

But in Boden's study, for those who developed a meth-use disorder, the researchers identified some other common characteristics that increased the chances of it happening, in addition to possessing the novelty-seeking trait. For example, if you were suffering from major depression or were without work while using, the odds of getting hooked increased. Being male, and having a parent who used illegal drugs or who was overly controlling all upped the odds of you becoming a heavy user. What's more, having adverse experiences as a child dramatically increases your odds of drug addiction later in life.

The overriding conclusion from ongoing research is that unhealed trauma was a major, if not *the* major, determinant in terms of who becomes addicted to drugs.

And the next offender is an example of this, where social circumstances and drugs can culminate in catastrophic consequences for the family at large and the entire town in which they live.

CHAPTER 9
'HORRIBLE, HORRIBLE MAN'
A Lethal Combination of Rage and Meth

THE VOLUNTEERS, WHO WERE KITTED OUT IN GUMBOOTS and raincoats and thermal layers, stoically continued their search, scouring the countryside in the relentless rain looking for any sign of the little girl who had simply disappeared without a trace from right outside the primary school gates.

Her stepdad had dropped her and her brother off at South Featherston School that morning, 9 September 2003, but, unlike her brother, she'd never made it to her classroom, and the alarm wasn't raised until 4 pm when she didn't get off the school bus and her mum reported her missing.

Within a matter of hours, her family and local community were turning out en masse to help look for six-year-old Coral Ellen Burrows. They dropped everything to join the police and search and rescue teams, combing through farmland and searching tree lines and buildings that surround the South Wairarapa countryside. Coral's biological dad hightailed it down from Te Puke to help look for her as soon as he heard she was missing.

The rain had turned normally lazy creeks into hazardous swift-flowing rivers, raising fears that Coral could have been swept away, so the police dive team was brought in to search the waters of Lake Wairarapa, while a helicopter joined in from above.

As the search continued, the media descended upon the small town of Featherston, population 1500, and locals told reporters they were holding on to hope that Coral may have just accidentally been locked in a barn somewhere and that she would be found safe and well. Dozens of trainee cops came in by bus from the Royal New Zealand Police College, going door to door, asking locals if they'd checked and double-checked their sheds and around their properties for Coral; had they seen anything, did they know anything at all that could help?

The Red Cross and Salvation Army kicked into gear, as did local businesses, ensuring that Coral's family and the search parties had ample supplies of food and wet weather gear. The hunt for the little girl went on for days, captivating the country's attention. One fella hitchhiked down from Hawke's Bay to help out, and it was said that when he held up his sign on the side of the road saying he was heading to Featherston to help look for Coral, motorists queued up to give him a ride. Another guy flew up from Christchurch to join the search party.

Coral's estranged parents, Jeanna Cremen and Ron Burrows, issued a public statement through the police saying the disappearance of their beloved daughter was every parent's worst nightmare. She was just a normal six-year-old kid who loved her dolls and getting cuddles and they urged the public to come forward with any detail they might have, no matter how small, in the hope it would help, be it an unusual car they'd seen, or a person who was acting suspiciously, or perhaps even a dog they recalled had been barking for no apparent reason. 'We love her, we miss her, we want her back,' they pleaded.

The police officer in charge of coordinating the search for Coral said he couldn't rule anything in or anything out in those first few days she was missing, including the possibility that foul play was involved. But local Featherston cops had a gut feeling from the second Coral was reported missing that her stepdad Steven Williams had something to do with it.

At just 29, Williams had already racked up a personal tally of around 90 convictions and he'd spent as much time inside youth and adult prisons as he had out of them.

He'd got off to a rough start in life, his dad had ditched the family when he was still a baby while his mum, Robyn, was a heavy drinker, with a temper, who had worked as a prostitute to make ends meet as Steven grew up. It wasn't unusual for her to be brazenly servicing clients in the family home. By age four, Steven was lighting fires and he was arrested for his first major crime, a home invasion, before he was even a teenager, then came the arsons, assaults, burglaries and kidnappings.

The cops in Featherston had been trying to take Williams down for a recent incident where they believed he'd shot at multiple people in the town after getting into a ruckus at a local bar, but they just couldn't make it stick.

To local law enforcement, Steven Williams had all the attributes of a ticking time bomb. Or, as one reporter put it, Williams' life always seemed destined to reach a grisly climax. 'His notoriously short fuse had got him in trouble so many times that those who knew him were resigned to the fact it was going to get worse.' The police had locked him up repeatedly over the years for various crimes and even called in the Armed Offenders Squad on one occasion to arrest him following an incident where he'd barricaded himself in his mum's home and armed himself with knives. Williams was known to grow cannabis but his drug use had escalated, as he'd recently begun using and selling methamphetamine.

When the police first spoke to him after Coral went missing, Williams told them he'd dropped her and her brother, Storm, off outside the school gate like normal and then spent a good chunk of the day visiting local dairy farms asking if they had any jobs going.

But he appeared reluctant to help search for his stepdaughter on that first evening. That night, as family and friends flocked to Coral's home to offer their support, Williams lay on the couch in the lounge with a blanket over his head. The following day, he did join the search for a few hours, but when interviewed a second time by the police, his story started to change, and it turned out he hadn't spent the day looking for work on local dairy farms after all. The real truth, Williams now told the detective, was that after dropping Coral at school he'd spent a good part of the day foraging for magic mushrooms in the Wairarapa countryside.

But after returning home that night, Williams began to have panic attacks and was taken to Masterton Hospital where he repeatedly smashed his head into a plate-glass window and was sedated. His erratic and self-destructive behaviour only increased the police's suspicion that Williams was involved in his stepdaughter's disappearance and they arrested him on other charges relating to previous crimes he'd committed, including trying to run down Jeanna's brother, Terry, in his Lada a few weeks earlier. Appearing in front of a judge the next day, Williams was remanded in custody and as he was led from the court to be taken to Rimutaka Prison, he flipped reporters the bird and gave them an angry spray for good measure as he was led away.

While the search teams kept on looking for Coral, day after day, determined to not give up hope of finding her, Williams was stewing in prison and after a week, he told a prison guard he wanted to make a confession. He'd killed Coral in a fit of rage and he was ready to tell the police exactly where she was. Later that night he led Detective Inspector Rod Drew to Coral's body, which he'd put in a sack and hidden in a big patch of giant toe toe grass just off a gravel track on the banks of Lake Ōnoke, which empties out into Palliser Bay, at the southern end of the North Island.

Williams broke down crying during his videoed police confession as he recounted how he'd panicked and thrown Coral's body into the bushes. 'What a horrible, horrible man I am,' he sobbed. 'I don't do things like this.' He claimed his memory was hazy about exactly what had happened, due to his rage and the methamphetamine, but it soon became clear exactly what he'd done. When Coral had refused to follow her brother and get out of the car outside the school that morning, Williams had flown into a violent rage, he'd swivelled around from the driver's seat and bashed her repeatedly, holding her little arm that was trying to deflect his blows with one hand while he rained down punches upon her with his other fist.

By the time he stopped hitting her, Coral's jaw was so badly broken the bone was sticking out of her face. Williams assumed she was dead and drove off to find somewhere to hide her body, but when he took her out of the car he heard her groan so he finished her off by bashing in her head with a thick branch he found nearby. He told the police he did that because he didn't want her to suffer.

On 19 September, ten days after she first went missing, the police announced they'd found Coral's body and that her stepfather, Steven Williams, had been charged with her murder.

As he appeared in court later that morning, an angry mob had gathered outside, hurling abuse at him. Coral's dad shouted out at him from the public gallery, 'Fry in hell, you piece of shit.'

A few days after Williams was sentenced to a minimum of 15 years in prison, Coral's mum gave an interview about the killing and the role she believed methamphetamine had played in it. She said Williams must have only started using P a few weeks before he killed her, and he must have been smoking it discreetly in the toilet or shower or something because as far as she could tell, he was still carrying on like normal, he was still making the kids their meals and still taking them to school, most of the time Steven was just his usual self – a happy clown.

But the family had received an unwelcome visitor. An aggrieved Black Power gang member called Junior had been to their house several times in the week before Coral's disappearance, menacing and threatening to shoot Williams, who'd sold him $300 worth of meth that apparently wasn't any good. Junior wanted his money back in full, but while they'd offered $80 to placate him, that just wasn't cutting it.

Williams was paranoid that Junior was going to make good on his threat, so he'd got himself a gun and stayed up around the clock for several days before he killed Coral, smoking P, waiting and watching for Junior to return.

Jeanna believes it was the combination of Steven's meth use and the stress of being hunted by Junior that culminated in Coral's death. Or as she put it to the reporter: 'Drugs is what killed my baby.'

Ron Burrows just doesn't buy that, though. He doesn't think methamphetamine had anything to do with Coral's murder and any suggestion that it did is just a total cop-out. Burrows said he had long been concerned that his kids were being abused in that home, he'd even phoned child protection services earlier that year trying to get them to investigate, and they did absolutely nothing. And, he points out, rather than getting help, Williams made the conscious decision to smash his daughter's head in instead.

As for Junior Kapene, the man who had been threatening Williams over a couple of hundred bucks of bad meth, he went on to become Black Power's New Zealand president and he confessed to a reporter years later that he remains haunted to this day by Coral's death, believing he's partly to blame. Kapene thinks that if Steven had not been so stressed and strung out fearing he was coming for him, he may not have flipped out and killed Coral. It's something he thinks about every single day.

Williams' lengthy prison sentence for killing Coral did nothing to temper his violent ways, and since then he's attempted to murder several other prisoners who crossed him behind bars. He poured boiling water over one inmate and then stabbed him repeatedly in the neck, believing he'd narked on him for having contraband tobacco. When appearing in court on that charge he took offense to the media.

'Fucking stare me down again, I'll fucking kill you,' he yelled at photographers.

In another attack Williams lured an inmate into a cell, stabbed him in the neck with a broken lightbulb, choked him unconscious and then stomped him and beat him with a broom. Following these brutal assaults, Williams would express his disappointment that he hadn't succeeded in killing the men.

* * *

In his 2015 book, *Chasing the Scream*, author Johann Hari explores the nature of drug addiction, quoting experts who show that childhood trauma and social circumstances play an enormous role in determining whether someone is likely to become addicted to a particular substance. Much more so than the addictive properties of the substance itself.

He discusses the Adverse Childhood Experiences Study, a huge project in America where researchers looked at a number of terrible things that can happen to a kid, such as being sexually molested, witnessing domestic violence in the house, growing up in a home with an alcoholic or having a parent in prison, and so on. They analysed how such events shaped the child's life. And they reached the conclusion that the current concept of addiction is ill-founded.

They established a scoring system: each time something bad happened to you, you would get a point, up to a maximum score of eight. In the study of 17,000 people, they found that every childhood trauma experienced sent the odds of that person becoming dependent on alcohol or tobacco or becoming an injector of drugs soaring. Some of the statistics gleaned from the study are eye-watering.

For example, a male child who scored a six, compared to a male child with a score of zero, was 46 times more likely to go on to inject a drug like methamphetamine at some point in their life.

Co-author, Dr Vincent Felitti, said it was proof that childhood trauma is a major determinant of who turns to drugs and becomes addicted, as the traumatised understandably, and yet often subconsciously, seek relief with psychoactive substances.

'Our findings are disturbing to some because they imply that the basic causes of addiction lie within us and the way we treat each other, not in drug dealers or dangerous chemicals,' he wrote.

* * *

Twenty years after Coral Burrows was brutally killed, I've travelled out to the remote Lake Ōnoke in southern Wairarapa to visit a memorial that has been placed here, to remember Coral. It is not far from where her battered little body was found in the toe toe bushes. A group of blokes from the Martinborough Men's Shed recently built the bench seat – locals felt the time was right for something a little more permanent out here, as a reminder and a tribute. Something to replace the informal shrine that had been operating for years, where people would come and tie teddy bears to a fence near the lake in her memory, because Coral had adored the soft cuddly toys.

I drive into the tiny township of Lake Ferry, which consists of a handful of houses, a small hotel and a campground, but I do a couple of laps up and down the road trying to spot the memorial site, without success.

It is a rubbish day today, and when I spot a local putting out her recycling on the roadside in her dressing gown, I pull over to ask her for directions. I also explain I'm working on a book about P – a subject she immediately tells me she wishes she didn't know so much about. And while she isn't sure where the memorial seat is, as she's only recently moved to the area, she is sure Mary the owner of the campground across the road who is due in at work shortly will know exactly where it is.

While we wait for Mary, this helpful Lake Ferry local invites me into her and her partner's home for coffee because she wants to tell me about the hell she and her family have been going through for most of the last 20 years because her son is hooked on meth.

Their lives have been 'non-stop chaos', with her boy in and out of rehab and prison like revolving doors since he was 19 years old. 'He keeps getting locked up,' she says, 'because he is constantly stealing in order to get more money to pay gangsters for more P.'

His modus operandi is to walk into supermarkets or big box stores like The Warehouse and simply walk right back out again with a trolley full of goods he hasn't paid for. If he is challenged by staff or store security, he simply shoves the trolley in one direction and runs off in the other, hoping they choose to give chase to their goods and not him. But the tactic isn't always successful and he's been locked up more times than his mum can remember — although she'll never forget the time her big stocky son was busted in the act of stealing women's leg razors to order — something that still makes her chuckle.

He's only recently come out of rehab for the umpteenth time and she says he is finally making a go of it; this time they hope he really will leave the meth behind.

As I said goodbye and thanks for the coffee I couldn't help thinking how you probably couldn't get much further away from the Golden Triangle or Mexican jungles than the seaside village of Lake Ferry, and yet the impacts of the meth being cooked and transported from there are very much being felt here.

I wander over to the campground where Mary Tipoki has now arrived and I receive directions to the memorial. I was on the wrong side of the lake. She says she can still clearly remember how locals had been so shocked when Coral's body was eventually found down by their lake after days of searching. It made it all the more raw that they knew the families involved too.

Before Coral's murder, Steven Williams's mum, Robyn, who was now a publican at a local bar, would occasionally visit the Lake Ferry Hotel, which Mary owns and ran at the time with her late husband, and Mary says she knows the Cremen family well also. Jeanna's dad, Tom Cremen, used to come down and drink in the hotel. Mary had been the first on the scene of his car accident where he ended up losing a leg. The Cremens were a wild bunch, she tells me.

She remembered how Jeanna had come down for a drink at the Lake Ferry Hotel not long after Coral was killed and was trying to hide her face from others in the bar. Mary went up and gave her a hug and followed up by writing a letter telling Jeanna just how sorry she was.

The strange thing is, Mary reflects, it was only shortly before Coral was killed that she'd heard about P for the first time at a local town meeting held in Wairarapa to highlight the dangers of meth.

Armed with Mary's fresh directions, I drive out of Lake Ferry and back across the rolling farmland the way I came, before turning down the East West Access Road and then taking another left into Western Lake Road. Steven Williams would eventually tell the police during his confession this was the route and the same roads he'd driven with Coral in the car on his way to dump her body.

After crossing a few one-way bridges on the dusty country road, I arrive at the entrance to Pounui, the Wairarapa Moana Wetlands Project, and I find Coral's bench seat. It looks out over the lake and Palliser Bay.

And as I sit on this wind-battered remote and lonely memorial to a young innocent victim, she is also a symbol of the violence and mayhem that surrounds this drug.

The placard on the memorial seat reads:

Coral Ellen Burrows
10.03.1997–09.09.2003
The place of our treasured girl.
Forever in our hearts.

CHAPTER 10

ZOMBIELAND
Media Campaigns and Scare-mongering

If the smoker is morose it will depress him more, and if he has homicidal tendencies it will cause him to commit murder. Even children will commit crimes of violence under the influence of marihuana.

The Gisborne Herald, 24 March 1950

SEVENTY YEARS AGO, NEW ZEALAND NEWSPAPERS CARRIED a report featuring a chilling warning about the threat that marijuana posed to decent society. It said it was the learned view of an Australian drug squad sergeant, who was presenting evidence in a Sydney court against a kitchenhand who had been caught with quarter of an ounce of this 'terrible' drug. Marihuana, the police officer said, was by far the worst drug that 'could be "let loose" on the community' for it removed every inhibition in the smoker, giving them full rein to carry out whatever deviant or criminal desires that should cross his mind. And with the cold hard facts laid bare, the young man was swiftly sentenced to 12 months hard labour in jail.

A decade earlier, *The New Zealand Herald* carried a column on marijuana which described it as 'the drug menace': 'More deadly than cocaine and opium, marihuana is the Devil's Drug that can be smoked in a harmless looking cigarette. It makes sober-minded young men and women irresponsible madcaps.'

Before marijuana, it was opium which was the boogeyman. For years, news of police raids on Chinese opium smokers around the country were routinely accompanied by headlines such as 'The Opium Evil' and 'The Opium Menace'. Then, while handing down the first prison sentence to a New Zealander for possessing LSD in 1965, Magistrate Luxford told the young Auckland freelance writer that 'the country had to stamp out the scourge of recreational drug taking' and accused him of 'fostering evil'. The 26-year-old from Parnell had been caught with 22 tabs of acid, less than 24 hours after a law change made it illegal; his lawyer urged the judge to take that into account. The lawyer also read to the court an excerpt from a book recently published in the United States that said the horrific pictures of disfigured acid users which had been circulating in the media were grossly exaggerated. But the magistrate wasn't having a bar of it. Anyone who would take LSD 'for kicks' was deliberately endangering themselves and helping to foster a nefarious public evil, he said, as he sent the writer to prison for six weeks.

In 1907, readers of the *Hawera & Normanby Star* newspaper were informed that the improper use of cocaine appeared to be spreading in New Zealand and that this had police and health officials worried. The article, titled 'The Drug Fiend', said cocaine users appeared to have their moral senses destroyed; 'it is believed that cocaine directly stimulates evil passions and evil deeds'. A few years later, the *Wanganui Chronicle* reported that Prime Minister William Massey was considering taking steps to combat 'the evil arising from the indiscriminate sale of such drugs as morphia and cocaine'.

And although the substance of most concern to society has regularly changed over the last century or so, the antiquated *Old Testament* treatment that drugs receive hasn't. Methamphetamine is still being described in exactly the same way as other drugs have been talked about in the past. Here's a selection of newspaper headlines over the last few years:

HOW NZ FELL PREY TO THE DEMON P

SCOURGE AND LEGACY OF EVIL DRUG TEARING AT OUR SOCIETY

METH PLAGUE AT RECORD LEVELS

BISHOP CALLS FOR ACTION OVER EVIL DRUG

NZ'S METH CRISIS – FIGHTING THE DEMON

METHAMPHETAMINE SCOURGE WILL BRING US TO OUR KNEES

When it comes to reporting on drugs it seems journalistic objectivity is non-existent. But it's not just a media problem: when the associate minister for health, Jim Anderton, reclassified meth as a Class-A drug in 2003, substantially increasing the penalties for supplying and manufacturing P, he said that what sets methamphetamine apart from other illegal drugs is that it is 'pure evil'. And it's not just a New Zealand phenomenon.

In Australia, where meth is similarly portrayed in the press, researchers have warned that the constant characterisation of the drug as evil simply cements the significant stigma that surrounds it and calcifies the existing discrimination against users. There's ample evidence that this acts as a barrier for users who genuinely need to seek treatment. Australian researchers have pointed out the extreme Christian symbolism routinely invoked when describing meth precludes any rational debate on the nature of the threat because there's only one rational response to evil – it must be stopped at all costs. They believe such portrayals of meth also push politicians into making law and order responses, rather than health-based ones.

Reporters might want to weigh this up the next time they think about describing P as an evil demon with insidious tentacles. In his book *Intoxicology: A Cultural History of Drink and Drugs*, author Stuart Walton examines the tendency of the press, police and politicians to treat every new drug that comes on to the street as the most gruesome and dangerous one yet, incredulous at the way each new 'lethal substance' is described as being more addictive and leading to even worse behaviour than the last.

'This is the drug's PR campaign, mounted for it by tabloid crime correspondents more gullible than any seasoned drug user would dare to be. The PR campaign for crack was a classic of its genre. One inhalation of it was said to addict the user for life, the obscene cravings that it created making heroin withdrawal look like nothing more than a sniffle.' In New Zealand, even still we're told that towns where meth use is common are 'cratered, as if having been hit by a meteorite', that meth wreaks chaos, pain and terror on anyone who gets in its way, that P is at epidemic and plague proportions, all despite official surveys showing meth use has fallen and remains relatively steady.

A few years back in 2017, one Kiwi reporter Paul Charman wrote an intriguing think piece questioning if it were time the country used its creative talents and launched a counter-offensive on P. It could possibly be along the lines of our famous 'ghost chips' anti drink-driving ad, he mused, but preferably a hard-hitting scare campaign perhaps not too dissimilar to the 1936 Hollywood classic *Reefer Madness*, which had warned the public of the insanity and depravity that came from smoking cannabis. Duly noting that *Reefer Madness* was so absurdly hyperbolic that it became a cult classic and actually encouraged cannabis use and also scorn for government anti-drug messages, the article said that P was so manifestly bad, it surely warranted similar shock treatment. After all, Charman positioned, the burglars climbing in through your windows to steal your stuff are either high on P or looking to sell your possessions to get some – and people shouldn't forget the power that art has to counteract evil.

There's certainly noble intent behind wanting to stop people becoming addicted to methamphetamine, but scare campaigns have been deployed against meth before.

* * *

As the two police officers escort a well-presented young man into the emergency department of an Australian hospital, he delivers, without warning, a savage head-butt to the face of the doctor who is greeting him. Using huge strength, the man, who was docile just seconds earlier, manages to throw the much larger police officers off him and hurl a chair into the glass window of the hospital's reception desk as the nurses behind it duck and scream in terror. He's finally subdued by multiple police officers and hospital security, and as the doctor checks if his own teeth are still in place, the voice-over states: 'Psychotic reactions can happen any time you use ice'.

That was the end scene of a 45-second ad produced by the Australian government in 2015 as part of its $9 million dollar anti-methamphetamine campaign, 'Ice Destroys Lives. Don't Let it Destroy Yours'. And the violence in the hospital was very much in keeping with the tone of the rest of the advertisements. In another scenario, an ice user elbows his mother in the face, knocking her to the floor in front of a young child – possibly his own – as she tries unsuccessfully to stop him taking money from her purse and leaving to get more drugs. Another young user digs her fingers deep into the flesh of her arm, the voice-over warning that some ice addicts believe bugs are crawling beneath their skin. The advertisement is narrated by Dr Stephen Priestley, the director of emergency medicine at Sunshine Coast Hospital, who tells Australians that, as an emergency doctor, 'I've seen people who can't sleep for days; people smoke it not realising it can be so addictive'.

But the campaign copped criticism on several fronts. For one, it was scene-for-scene if not word-for-word identical to another Australian anti-ice campaign launched in 2007; and two, experts warned that the ads were not only hyperbolic but also that fear-based advertising fuels stigma and drives people away from, rather than towards, seeking treatment. One Australian alcohol and drug expert wrote that the ad campaign was typical of the tendency of the Australian government and the media to incite unnecessary fear and misinform the public about this 'supposed menace'. It is crucial that ice use and harm is accurately portrayed so services and responses can be appropriately targeted, they said.

However, a group of researchers surveyed 1000 Australians about the 'Ice Destroys Lives' campaign and found the ads were widely recognised and that three-quarters of those who had seen them said it made them not want to try ice. So, on the one hand, apparently successful.

But those who have previously used crystal methamphetamine had a very different take on the ads. They felt 'Ice Destroys Lives' misrepresented and greatly exaggerated the nasty side of the drug; they said the campaign used negative stereotyping to unfairly portray people who use ice as being violent and crazy, and it would not encourage them to seek help.

Matt Noffs is the chief executive of the Noffs Foundation, Australia's largest youth drug and alcohol treatment service provider, and in his book *Breaking the Ice*, he says a global narrative has emerged around methamphetamine where its users are deliberately dehumanised. He's accused the Australian media of being 'ice mad' at times, pointing to coverage such as a column in which an alleged ice user was described as being 'no longer human' and 'whose eyes screamed "I have no soul"'. Other Aussie articles have contentiously blamed ice addiction for a mentally disturbed young woman chewing off her toes, and another for a young man gouging out and then proceeding to eat his own eyes. Then there is the smattering of stories in Australia in which ice users are reported to obtain superhuman strength, able to fight off multiple police, security officers and hospital staff trying to restrain them.

Superhuman strength is a quality attributed to most recreational drugs at some point. One of the Los Angeles police officers involved in the arrest and beating of motorist Rodney King who was pulled over for speeding, which sparked the deadly LA riots in 1992, told investigators they believed he was high on PCP. As the sergeant stood by watching his police colleagues take turns beating King with their clubs and tasering him, he said he was recalling with fear the stories of how PCP gave people superhuman strength, and feared King could have 'turned into The Hulk at any moment' and placed officers in a death grip.

Meanwhile, in the southern United States in 1914, police officers swapped out their standard revolvers for higher calibre weapons in order to combat a new menace: 'crazed negro cocaine fiends', whose use of the drug was said to make them impervious to bullets that would stop sane men dead in their tracks. This followed a fight in which a North Carolina police chief was said to have placed the muzzle of his gun 'over a negro's heart' and fired, 'intending to kill him right quick', but neither that shot nor the next one to his chest even staggered him. The police chief did eventually manage to beat the man to death with his club, however. From the fears about Chinese and their opium, or black Americans and cocaine, to the grossly disproportionate prosecution of Māori for drug offences today, the war on drugs has always gone hand-in-hand with racism, and we'll soon see some more examples of this.

* * *

The Australian government's graphic ad campaign to scare off potential users of ice looks like a Disney cartoon compared to the shock approach taken by an anti-meth campaign that's been running in the United States for nearly 20 years: as a dad pulls up and his teenage daughter hops into the backseat of his car, she looks somewhat surprised and questions where her mum is. Her dad doesn't respond but just stares straight ahead and drives to a dark industrial area. Here, he stops and gets out of the car and is handed a bag of methamphetamine from his dealer. His daughter cries out to her dad for help as the meth dealer climbs into the backseat with her. She realises the child-lock is on and she can't get out. 'I never wanted this life for her,' her father says in the voice-over, while the car rocks up and down behind him, his dealer clearly raping his daughter, 'but here I am, feeling more dead than alive.'

It's just one of the many explicit and disturbing ads that are part of the Montana Meth Project's unapologetic campaign to terrify teenagers about crystal meth. They regularly broadcast graphic footage and images of meth users tearing at and digging into their own flesh; teenage girls prostituting themselves for as little as $15 so they can score another hit; meth-crazed kids robbing and beating their parents for meth money.

In another, a young woman cries as she looks in the bathroom mirror, and water runs into the sink. She poses this question to herself: 'If I had asked, "What does meth do to your brain, does it make you hear voices?" Or if I'd asked, "Can't you just stop doing meth?" my mum wouldn't be asking …'

Her mum: 'What did you do?' The mother has entered the bathroom and is aghast as she sees the deep cuts across her daughter's wrists and tries to grab towels to stem the blood as it pours into the bathroom sink and onto the floor.

'We are the unwavering voice of meth prevention', the Montana Meth Project website states, an unwavering voice that assures you that trying meth just once leads you down a path to guaranteed addiction, where appalling acts of degradation and violence will become the norm, where you're almost guaranteed to end up terribly disfigured by unsightly facial sores.

The Project got off the ground in 2005 when self-made billionaire Thomas Siebel decided to make it his mission to scare kids off crystal meth. His hunting buddy was a local sheriff and every time they went out together, the sheriff would tell him how much worse the meth problem was becoming in Montana. Siebel heard how almost 50 per cent of those in Montana jails were incarcerated because of meth-related crimes, and over half of those parents whose children were taken from them and placed in foster homes had been using meth. Siebel decided to do something about it – and he doesn't do things by halves.

In an interview with US business magazine *Fast Company*, Siebel told reporter James Verini that in the first two years of the Montana Meth Project, he spent $26 million dollars on the campaign, funding 45,000 ads on television, 35,000 radio ads, 10,000 print ads and 1000 billboards. James Verini wrote that as he drove to the interview, he passed one of those billboards. It had a close-up image of a teenage girl with meth mouth – her rotting teeth and blistered lips on full display, beneath a caption that read: YOU'LL NEVER WORRY ABOUT LIPSTICK ON YOUR TEETH AGAIN.

The goal for Montana Meth Project was total saturation, and they became the biggest advertiser in the state. They brought in top directors to film and produce their advertisements and run their campaigns, and Siebel was remorseless about terrifying teenagers because, in his eyes, there's no question about it, meth really is the perfect drug to rally against.

'With all of these other things – cocaine, alcohol, marijuana – there are some positive effects. You can relax. You can concentrate. I'd even argue there are some positive effects to cigarettes. Meth has no positive effects. It's such an easy product to work with,' Siebel explained.

And Montana Meth Project is more than just a jolting ad campaign, it has organised public art competitions across the state, while in neighbouring Idaho, thousands of teenagers have painted anti-meth murals to be plastered everywhere, on the sides of buildings and buses, to dumpsters, grain silos and even on cows and sheep. Montana teenagers wear their free Meth Project merchandise: sunglasses and wristbands sporting the campaign's slogan 'Not Even Once', and the website features an array of wallpapers to download onto your computer or phone screen, featuring tortured-looking meth users. It also offers online tutorials that schools can access to scare their students straight.

Other states have come on board, with the Meth Project rolled out in Arizona, Colorado, Georgia, Idaho, Montana, Hawaii and Wyoming. Siebel claims their campaign has been 'terrifically successful', pointing to a 77 per cent reduction in teen methamphetamine use in Montana since the project launched and the lowest-ever reported rates of meth use among

Native American teens in the state, and equally impressive outcomes in the other states too.

But others aren't quite so sure. While Montana's teen meth use did indeed fall in the years following its launch, teen meth use right across the United States has been on the decline since peaking in the early 2000s. What's more, just like in New Zealand, Montana authorities had changed the rules, meaning you could no longer obtain pseudoephedrine over the counter at pharmacies, making it much harder to make meth, while police had also cracked down on methamphetamine. An Australian researcher who analysed these claims of success and who delved into the Meth Project's own data came to the conclusion that Montana teens' views on meth had barely changed, and the number of teens 'strongly disapproving' of meth had actually fallen from 98 per cent before the ads started running in 2005 to 91 per cent in 2008.

Similarly, Professor Mark Anderson at Montana University's department of economics looked into the Meth Project. He found that, after considering the pre-existing downward trend in crystal meth use, the campaign had had no discernible impact on methamphetamine use whatsoever. Anderson looked at seven other US states that had adopted the Meth Project and what impact it had had on meth use. After reviewing the national and state's youth risk-behaviour surveys, which ask students about things like their exercise and eating habits, violence, sexuality and their substance use, he again found the Meth Project was having little if any impact.

'It is apparent that meth use has been trending smoothly downward in all states during the period under study. If the

Meth Project had an effect, then we would expect to see an acceleration of this trend as states began adopting the campaign … if anything, the decrease in meth use appears to have slowed among adopting states after 2005, the inaugural year of the Meth Project in Montana.'

For Dr Carl Hart, an outspoken US neuroscientist who specialises in what recreational drugs do to the brain, says what we're seeing now with the way meth is portrayed has all the hallmarks of the hysteria that surrounded the crack cocaine crisis in the United States in the 1980s. Crack cocaine, which is cocaine turned into rock form so it can be smoked, was made out to be vastly more dangerous and addictive than powder cocaine, which is most often snorted, but can be swallowed or injected too. At the height of the crack panic, one puff of the drug was said to cause instant addiction, crack was said to be a major driver of crime, psychosis and death, and there were endless reports of it corrupting and ruining the poor, predominantly black, communities where crack was prevalent. The relentless coverage of its dangers led to politicians introducing vastly harsher criminal penalties for crack users and suppliers than for those of cocaine powder, despite it being exactly the same drug.

The 1986 Anti-Drug Abuse Act, drafted by then Senator Joe Biden, introduced a mandatory minimum five-year sentence for anyone trafficking 5 grams of crack or 500 grams of cocaine: a 100-fold difference. But as then-presidential candidate Barack Obama noted many years later, the only real difference between cocaine and crack was the skin colour of the user, and later as president, he began shrinking the sentencing disparity between the two substances.

In December 2022, the US Attorney-General announced that the now President Joe Biden and his government would completely remove the crack versus cocaine powder disparity, saying it had no basis in science and simply fuelled unwarranted racial disparities in sentencing.

Dr Hart says exactly the same scaremongering is being invoked around meth. For example, the Montana Meth Project and its spinoffs claim meth is instantly addictive, media stories hone-in on the worst-case scenarios and publish exaggerated claims of a meth epidemic, a police captain warns the public that meth 'makes crack look like child's play'.

After reviewing the existing scientific literature on methamphetamine, Hart published a paper that challenged a lot of the conventional research done on methamphetamine. Unconventional, and described as a 'rockstar advocate' for drug decriminalisation, Hart has been open about his own recreational drug use and believes responsible adults should be free to use drugs if they choose to. He feels other researchers in this field have often been too quick to attribute negative outcomes to meth use, and that sloppily designed studies have led to bogus claims, such as that meth use irreversibly diminishes intelligence and impairs cognitive function. He says the science is clear, that small to moderate doses of methamphetamine boost performance, improve mood and reduce tiredness.

All the things you'd typically expect from a stimulant. But it's at high doses, and particularly repeated high doses of P, where it proves problematic. When it gets to the point that it's severely disrupting the user's sleep, it has been shown to cause psychological disturbances including paranoia and psychosis in some users. One of Hart's key pieces of advice for new meth users is to consider swallowing the drug rather than smoking or injecting it because, just like cocaine, those methods produce more potent effects.

Another problem with the 'end is nigh' reporting on meth, he argues, is that there's another drug, which has almost identical effects to methamphetamine, is widely used, and comes with almost none of the controversy: d-amphetamine.

D-amphetamine, also called dextroamphetamine and which is sold as Dexedrine, is a key ingredient in ADHD drugs like Adderall and its generic versions, for which there were more than 40 million prescriptions issued in the United States in 2021 alone. Both drugs are central nervous system stimulants that boost the amount of dopamine in the brain. When people have been given the same-sized doses of methamphetamine or d-amphetamine during research trials, the effects are incredibly similar: their blood pressure and pulse rise, they report feeling more awake and alert, they're talkative, happy and have a sense of euphoria.

While some participants' hearts thumped a little harder and faster when given the meth, and they rated their 'high' a little higher, overall there was very little difference in how they were affected. Meth and d-amphetamine, while molecularly different, are essentially the same drug. In some countries, New Zealand included, methamphetamine has been banned, even for medical purposes, yet they still allow d-amphetamine to be used. And given their similarities, Hart has taken a swing at the so-called 'meth mouth' campaign, pointing out both meth and d-amphetamine restrict saliva-flow, causing what's informally called dry mouth, and yet there are no campaigns about 'Adderall mouth' or reports linking it to extreme tooth decay. The dental issues experienced by some methamphetamine users, he believes, are much more likely to be linked to poor sleep and nutrition and a lack of dental hygiene than meth itself.

Despite the campaigns around meth advertising that it is extremely addictive, Hart's research says other evidence is clear: the overwhelming majority of people who take meth will do so without a problem, and less than 15 per cent of users will ever become addicted.

Even so, this still appears to be a fairly decent-sized risk that if you use methamphetamine, things can go pear-shaped.

* * *

Matt Noffs argues that the recurring theme in Australia's media coverage has been to paint ice users as the enemy – it's us against them – a public portrayal he calls the 'zombification' of meth users. While he acknowledges heavy meth use can occasionally lead to aggressive behaviour, paranoia and psychosis, he believes this is all the more reason for focusing on harm-reduction initiatives, such as drug consumption rooms, where users can inject and, in some cases, inhale their drugs like methamphetamine under the supervision of trained medical staff.

In an interview with Radio New Zealand in 2016, Noffs said that in the previous four years, around 80,000 people had injected ice in the Kings Cross, Sydney, injection room and there hadn't been a single episode of violence. Drug-consumption rooms are increasingly common in countries like Germany where, in addition to giving people a safe, nonjudgemental place to use, the often-impoverished drug users are able to access other support services, medical and social, and which advocates say frequently puts them on a pathway to improving their situation.

Sydney's injection room was opened 20 years ago – an official response to the hundreds of heroin users who were injecting on the streets in the city, leaving it littered with needles and, not-infrequently, corpses. On its twentieth anniversary in 2021, the Kings Cross injection room had overseen 1.2 million injections, there had been more than 10,000 overdoses on site, none of which resulted in a death, while the staff who worked there had made almost 19,000 referrals to health and other services for its customers. Noffs reckons it's time New Zealand got on board and set up consumption rooms of their own for P.

Another expert who's been highly critical of the coverage of methamphetamine, especially in her native Australia, is Dr Nicole Lee, an advisor to the Aussie government on drug and alcohol policy. She believes a lot of the commentary around ice is driven by fear over the facts and that the exaggerated language and imagery surrounding ice succeeds only in building a wall of stigma that acts as a barrier for those needing treatment.

Dr Lee says the real facts are that the vast majority of people who use meth each year will do so only a few times, and while they may feel flat for a day or two after using, their dopamine levels will quickly return to normal; in other words, for most people she'll be right, mate. These occasional users will naturally choose to stop using at some point. But, at the other end of the scale, you have the hardcore users, around 15 per cent, who will consume ice multiple times a week and in high doses, and it's these people who suffer vastly higher risks of dependence and harm.

When you take meth, it sends the dopamine in your brain soaring and the current understanding, Nicole Lee explained to me, is that excess dopamine is linked to psychosis – people with schizophrenia, for example, have higher levels of dopamine markers. If you're constantly pumping huge amounts of dopamine into your brain and you're constantly wired, the odds of having a bad outcome rise fast.

In his book *Riding with the Devil, Me and 'P': the Lisa Cropp Story*, sports journalist Mike Dillon was openly disdainful of all drugs but especially methamphetamine, which he variously described as hideous, a villain and the world's most serious drug.

He claimed that most murders in recent times were attributable to P, and concluded that his hatred for methamphetamine had only grown as he learned more about the drug while writing the book. He condemned what he saw as New Zealand's inadequate penalties for using or supplying methamphetamine, slamming many of the prison sentences handed down for P as a joke and pointing admiringly to the much tougher penalties in Canada and Malaysia – the latter, he wrote, employs the death penalty in such cases.

In footage posted to TikTok by a Malaysian news outlet, the harrowing cries of Hairun Jalmani, a distraught 55-year-old single mother of nine, can be heard as she is led, handcuffed, from a court room by a police officer. She is wailing and pleading for help, asking who will look after her children. Jalmani, a poor fishmonger, had just been sentenced to death by hanging. She'd been caught three years earlier in 2018 with just over 100 grams of methamphetamine; until mid-2022, being caught with more than 50 grams brought with it a mandatory death sentence in the country.

Amnesty International Malaysia condemned her sentence saying it reflected how Malaysia's death penalty punishes the poor and particularly discriminates against women, that Jalmani's life chances were stacked against her as a single mother in the country's poorest state, trying to support her children. She would be joining 135 other women on death row in Malaysia, 95 per cent of them there for drug trafficking, most commonly meth.

According to a study carried out by researcher Dr Lucy Harry at the Centre for Criminology at Oxford University, the majority of the condemned female prisoners in Malaysia were foreigners from less-affluent neighbouring countries like Thailand, Philippines and Indonesia, women who were either unemployed or in precarious employment when caught smuggling. And although some knowingly take the risks in order to try to get some quick money and make ends meet, others genuinely believe they've been recruited for jobs as domestic workers in Malaysia and are tricked and deceived into carrying luggage there with them.

One lawyer recounted to Dr Harry an account of their client in this situation who was now on death row. She had never travelled before. She didn't even own a suitcase; she had turned up at the place where she would collect a ticket to Malaysia holding plastic carrier bags with her clothes in them. The person who offered her a job as a masseuse gave her a bag to take with her to Malaysia, and once she arrived in the country she was supposed to drop that bag off at a particular address to a particular person. She had all of this information in a text message. So, she accepted the bag, put her clothes into it, and travelled to Malaysia. When she arrived, the X-ray showed something suspicious in the bag, and drugs were found in the lining.

Some of the women sentenced to death report being paid about US$500 to transport their bags or suitcases into Malaysia and many are adamant they never knew what was in them. Hardly drug kingpins, just impoverished women and unwitting drug mules, now possibly about to pay the ultimate price.

CHAPTER 11

STRAIGHT SHOOTING
Needle Exchanges and Drug Checking in New Zealand

ON A FROSTY WINTER'S MORNING IN 2021, I MADE MY WAY along Wellington's bustling Lambton Quay packed with children and their parents, in the middle of the July school holidays, to a discreet office on Willis Street that happens to be the home of the capital's needle-exchange programme.

As you enter the front door you come to a vending machine stocked with an array of injecting equipment that can be accessed 24 hours a day. There are needles, syringes, filters, tourniquets, sterile water and other equipment to help users inject safely. To the left of the vending machine is a sturdy yellow recycling box where users can dispose of their used needles and syringes.

About 35 years ago, in the face of the global HIV epidemic, the New Zealand government passed ground-breaking legislation to set up the first state-sponsored needle-exchange programme in the world. As Health Minister Michael Bassett put it at the time: 'Don't inject, seek treatment, but if you do inject, never share needles – buy your own.' And the programme proved to be unquestionably successful – with just 0.2 per cent of the New Zealanders who inject drugs contracting HIV compared to a global rate of 13 per cent (and in parts of Russia more than 30 per cent of injecting drug users have the virus).

In 2020 a study published by Auckland University found that between 1996 and 2018, Aotearoa was averaging just one HIV diagnosis per year among people injecting drugs and one of the report's authors, Dr Geoff Noller, said there was simply no question that this was attributable to the success of the needle-exchange programme. 'It's an example of the harm-reduction approach to drug use, which seeks to work alongside people to improve their health and wellbeing without coercion, judgement or discrimination,' he wrote.

Not only does the programme give drug injectors an endless supply of fresh needles, meaning they don't need to be shared or reused, it also dramatically reduces thefts of needles and syringes from hospitals. A government review of the programme back in 2002 found it had prevented 20 deaths, 2000 cases of HIV/AIDS and Hepatitis C, and saved the country around 35 million dollars in treatment costs.

Two decades on and I sit with the Wellington Needle Exchange centre manager, Debbie Whiting, and general manager, Carl Greenwood. Both explain the life paths that led them to work here.

For Carl, growing up in New Zealand as a gay man in the 1970s and early '80s when it was still illegal wasn't easy, to put it mildly. He'd always used cannabis to help escape from reality before he himself escaped even further – to London, where he began working 70-hour weeks. And when his mates invited out him out clubbing one night, they wouldn't take his being knackered as an excuse not to go, offering him some speed to help get him through. Which began Carl's love affair with hard drugs because, as he told me, who needs to sleep when you can just snort speed. Pretty soon, it was his weekly norm – speed was on the menu most Fridays and Saturdays and then ecstasy arrived on the scene, the parties becoming giant lovefests. But in 1989 Carl received an HIV diagnosis and his partner passed away three years later in 1992. At just 27 years old, the medical experts told Carl he had just ten years to live, tops.

With that seeming death sentence hanging over his head, Carl decided he could sleep when he was dead, and so began a ten-year bender. Along with many others who had similar diagnoses, they did lots of drugs, went clubbing as much as they could, cashed in their life insurance policies and lived incredibly hedonistic, debauched lifestyles. There were drugs trips to Asia, a pound of cannabis smoked in North Sumatra, shrooms were on the menu in Thailand along with pharmaceuticals like Valium, and after years of partying in London and abroad, Carl made his way to Melbourne in 1998.

But his body was starting to pack up and he went to see an HIV specialist who told him about a new therapy trial of antiretroviral drugs, and once on them, luckily for Carl there was some immediate success. While his health improved, Carl's drug habit didn't. By now he'd started to inject drugs; he'd snorted so much cocaine over the years that the pain in his nose was too intense, so he was shooting up instead.

Then, in 1999, Carl's drug dealer swung by for his weekly visit with a bag of crystal meth that he asked Carl to try and give him an honest review. His dealer was wanting to know if he should start stocking ice (as they call it in Australia). The next week Carl told his dealer he never wanted anything else ever again, all he wanted now was meth, it was incredible, not only could it quickly be dissolved in water and injected but it also delivered a far bigger rush than speed ever had. The buzz lasted a lot longer too, and for the next five years Carl used heavily. He thinks his HIV medication interacted with the meth somehow giving him longer-lasting highs – not that he ever mentioned his drug use to his doctors. There was too much stigma to do that, he said, too much shame. He recalls one blood test when a nurse saw his bruised vein and recoiled, horrified. She warned her needle was going to hurt, and she made sure it did.

In 2004, Carl was working at Melbourne's Royal Children's Hospital as a purchasing officer for the kitchen, a glorified storeman, as he puts it, and he was starting to feel like he'd had enough. He was now spending more on meth than he was earning, he was shooting up in order to get out the door and make it to work on Monday mornings, he'd burned through his annual leave and his sick leave, he was exhausted, the meth was in control and the drug had lost its appeal.

But it wasn't just the drugs that were getting to him. Until 1998, Carl had simply assumed he'd be dead within a few years; by 2005 and now in his forties, it was clear that with the new HIV medication, he had a future and quite possibly decades to live. All of a sudden he realised he could well live to 65, and his whole perspective on life started changing. So he returned to New Zealand to detox, and after a short stint at his parents' house on the Kāpiti Coast, he moved in with a friend in Kaikōura. She was mourning the recent loss of her husband while Carl was mourning the loss of his drugs. Because in Kaikōura, in 2005, scoring meth was out of the question.

He wasn't aware of any official rehab programmes in place back then; if there were he hadn't heard of them. Meth was still too new, but he doesn't think they would have worked for him anyway. The way Carl broke his meth habit was by substituting it for pot – every time he thought about meth he'd simply get stoned, day after day, week after week. And it worked for him. It's part of the beef he has with modern-day rehab programmes, which he says mostly revolve around abstinence from all substances. For most users, you have to pass a drug test just to be accepted into the programme, but it's not the way it works for everyone.

Carl got a job as a manager at the local New World supermarket, and while he struggled with his mental health and felt suicidal at times, he put his head down and found the job gave him much-needed routine and structure. After about a year there, he felt pretty good. He said his brain started working properly again, his natural dopamine started to kick in and he was feeling pretty fine. He also knew it was high time to get out of Kaikōura, so he headed back to Wellington and got a job with the AIDS Foundation, and then in 2012 began working at Needle Exchange.

For Debbie Whiting, she explained that she'd never injected, herself, but had spent her fair share of time partying with speed and cocaine in Sydney in the late 1980s and early 1990s. Having a drug dealer living in her apartment helped ensure a steady supply, and amphetamines in particular she found to be fantastic – you could go hard all weekend and when you're feeling flat on Monday morning, one quick line and you're off to work feeling great all over again, she said.

Debbie felt like she could cope with anything while on speed. She was simply bloody firing on all cylinders and able to give everything 110 per cent – whether it be dancing, drinking or working. But she reconsidered her hobby after a series of nosebleeds saw her visit her doctor, who asked Debbie to answer honestly as to whether she was snorting cocaine or speed, to which she replied, 'Yeah, shitloads of it.'

The purity of the drugs were destroying the membranes and cartilage in her nose the doctor warned her, telling her she needed to stop snorting drugs. For Debbie it was a bit of a wake-up call.

But her affair with amphetamines finished for good when she returned to live in Whanganui in 1992 and her friends just about laughed her out of the house when she enquired about finding some speed or cocaine locally.

You'd be bloody lucky to even find some pot around here, they said.

Now Debbie and Carl, wearing their 'Support Don't Punish' jumpers, see themselves as activists fighting against the stigma and discrimination around drug use. And there's an awful lot of shame surrounding methamphetamine, they feel, where many of the public are repulsed by meth's reputation, which means users in turn are ashamed. Add to that the criminal penalties and the constant threat of arrest bringing 24/7 paranoia, as well as alienation for users, they all become barriers for seeking help. Carl and Debbie think around half of their customers in the capital are using meth, with Ritalin, methadone and morphine rounding out the top four most-injected substances. At the Napier site, in comparison, they believe about 80 per cent of the customers are injecting meth.

Once you inject meth, they say, it's very hard to go back to snorting and smoking it, because the rush you get is simply 'off the charts' in comparison. At the moment, the needle-exchange programme acts as a harm-reduction service for those who inject drugs, but as staff, they really have no contact with more recreational users or those or snort or smoke or ingest the drug. They reckon if they were allowed to sell glass pipes and snorting straws, they'd be able to get the harm-reduction messages out there to a much higher number of methamphetamine users.

The walls of the centre are covered in posters and pamphlets with facts and harm-reduction information about drugs – pamphlets about methamphetamine and how it affects your body, its dangers, and tips on how to stay healthy when using, like keeping hydrated, eating food even if you're not particularly hungry, remembering to brush your teeth and cleaning any sores with antiseptic solution so they don't get infected. There are pamphlets explaining which filters to match with which drug you're injecting (filtering drugs removes their impurities and contaminants and reduces the damage you do your body); there are others on how to inject safely and when to seek medical advice if you get an infection. There is information giving advice on how to look after your veins – veintenance – and there's specific guidance on injecting meth and opioids too.

I asked Carl and Debbie what steps they would take, if it were up to them, to reduce the harm caused by methamphetamine use in New Zealand. They said their first step would be to decriminalise it. Their logic: if people can't be honest about their drug use from the start, which is hard when it's illegal, you're never going to get ideal health outcomes. As long as it's illegal, everything will always stay underground, whereas at least with decriminalisation, you can create a platform in society where people can come forward and talk about their meth use without risking a knock on the door from the police.

Their second step would be to legalise methamphetamine entirely and turn drug use from a criminal justice issue into a health issue. Carl believes it would be great if you could just purchase the drug from your local pharmacy, just like you used to be able to in New Zealand 60 years ago. It would remove the chaos of people having to chase black-market drugs all day, it'd give them structure and allow them to find work and bring a sense of normality back to their lives. If meth is here to stay, and it certainly looks like it is, then we have to think of different ways to deal with it, Carl explains. Prohibition hasn't worked, all the drugs are still here, and prohibition makes it difficult for people to find good health outcomes.

In 2020, the needle-exchange programme distributed more than three million needles and syringes across a network of 21 dedicated exchanges and 200 support partner-pharmacies across the country. Then on World Hepatitis Day in 2021, the government boosted funding so they could supply more injection equipment in a bid to eradicate Hepatitis C as a major health threat by 2030. Commonly spread by injecting drugs, Hepatitis C leads to liver disease and cancer; associate Health Minister Ayesha Verrall estimated around 45,000 New

Zealanders have the virus but only about half of them know it. She said many of those with the virus come from our most marginalised communities, and face significant barriers to getting tested and treated, including the stigma that surrounds their activities and the virus.

I'd actually met Carl Greenwood two years earlier when he was voicing his frustration to a parliamentary select committee about the fact that police were still arresting and charging hundreds of their customers each year for possession of needles – more than 30 years after the needle-exchange programme was brought in and the law changed to specifically allow people to possess needles and syringes if they purchased them through the programme.

Apart from providing an obvious incentive for those injecting drugs to discard their used needles immediately and possibly recklessly rather than returning them to be recycled responsibly, such police action heaped more stigma and discrimination upon users, Carl said, in my follow-up story for *1News*. Former associate Health Minister Peter Dunne agreed that the police behaviour beggared belief and accused them of deliberately undermining the needle-exchange programme as many of the charges are eventually dropped anyway if the person arrested obtains a letter from a needle exchange centre showing they purchased or acquired their equipment from them.

And as we sat there talking at Needle Exchange in Wellington, a small number of customers entered the shop to purchase needles and syringes – all part of this world-leading harm-reduction initiative – and yet they still run the risk of being arrested for doing so. It seems Michael Bassett's message from 1987 about never sharing needles but to buy your own still hasn't really filtered through to Police HQ or his political descendants, who have refused to remove this offence from legislation.

* * *

It was New Year's Day 2019 and I was working through the summer break, when Police Minister Stuart Nash texted me to say he was on his way up to the iconic Rhythm & Vines music festival in Gisborne where thousands of young New Zealanders had been partying, to announce that he wanted to legalise pill checking.

The organisers had issued an alert to the party-goers during the festival that their security guards had intercepted some ecstasy, which had been cut with a pesticide. Nash, whose daughter and friends were regular attendees at music festivals, thought it was unacceptable that those purchasing drugs at these sorts of festivals had no way of knowing if the pill they were going to swallow or powder they were about to snort would lead to the best time of their life or an overdose and potentially death.

And so, as those at Rhythm & Vines packed up their tents around him, Nash told the public that while 20,000 young people had had a great time in Gisborne, he wanted drug testing at festivals to become the norm. 'I think it saves lives, it saves hospitalisation, it's actually the right thing to do. And it's dealing with the reality in which we find ourselves.'

In contrast, across the ditch in Australia, police operating at festivals take a very different approach to young people taking ecstasy and other drugs: they frequently deploy drug-detector dogs to monitor the entrances and walk the dogs through the crowds themselves. In effect, it is a harm-*maximisation* policy as it sends a clear message to festival goers that they should swallow all of their drugs before they arrive at the gates. Researchers have found that not only do Aussie festival goers wolf down their drugs at the first sign of sniffer dogs but also that the police routinely strip-search anyone that a sniffer dog indicates has drugs on them, leaving many people feeling violated and traumatised.

Some New South Wales police were investigated by the Law Enforcement Conduct Commission for repeatedly strip-searching teenagers, one as young as 12 years old, at festivals, and in some cases touching their bottoms and closely inspecting their genitals. Also disturbingly, in many cases the young Australians have no support person with them and most of them have no drugs on them either. And that's because a drug-detection dog's strike rate is pretty damn hopeless.

An investigation by the Australian ombudsman in 2006 into the use of sniffer dogs in NSW looked at more than 10,000 cases where drug-detection dogs had indicated someone was possessing drugs and that person was then searched: in 74 per cent of cases, no drugs were found. In South Australia in 2018, in more than 80 per cent of cases where sniffer dogs had indicated a positive finding, no drugs were found on that person.

The director of a private dog-training company, Dog Force Australia, told Aussie media that the reason there are so many seemingly false IDs is that a dog's sense of smell is so sensitive it will positively identify anyone who has been in the vicinity of illegal drugs – people who have touched drugs recently perhaps, or even someone who has bank notes on them with traces of drugs on them.

One in five Aussies who were strip-searched by the police and found to have no drugs on them said people had been smoking pot near them – which at a festival isn't surprising.

Back home, Stuart Nash's New Year's resolution to legalise drug-checking services quickly hit a snag when the Labour Party's coalition partner, New Zealand First, initially stymied the move. Its law-and-order spokesperson Darroch Ball told me that pill testing blurs the lines between what is right and what is wrong, what's legal and illegal. The key to preventing harm, he said, was simply to stop young people from taking drugs in the first place.

Right.

But New Zealand First was on the wrong side of public opinion as support for pill-checking services to be legalised in New Zealand was enormous. In late 2019, *1News* polled 1000 New Zealanders on whether drug-checking services should be legal: 75 per cent were for it; just 19 per cent were opposed.

At their political conference that year in Christchurch, New Zealand First's youth wing challenged the elders over their opposition to pill checking, urging them to employ some common sense. It was a 'no brainer' pill testing should be legal, William Woodward told the party's MPs, and it wasn't about encouraging drug use, he said, it was about saving lives. To their credit, New Zealand First listened. Meanwhile, National, as opposition, steadfastly ignored similar calls from its youth wing, the Young Nats, who believed drug checking would save lives; National's leader Simon Bridges was adamant it sent the wrong message.

The right message being that drugs are bad, mkay?

With the governing parties Labour, New Zealand First and the Green Party all on board, temporary legislation was swiftly brought in to enable legal pill-checking be in place for the summer of 2020.

A few months after visiting the Needle Exchange, I watched as dozens of young Wellingtonians, wearing face masks and forming an orderly, socially distanced queue, lined up outside a nondescript office building waiting their turn to have their black-market drugs tested and checked. With just a week to go before New Year, it was their last opportunity to find out if what they'd bought was the real McCoy or a potentially dangerous alternative.

Over the course of the next two hours, several dozen 20-somethings caught the lift up to the Drug Foundation's office on the fourth floor and handed over the drugs they'd purchased to the volunteers and staff of the drug-checking organisation, Know Your Stuff. They would return half an hour later for their results. There, the team took a tiny sample of the drug, that day ketamine, LSD and MDMA were brought in, and they ran it through a $50,000 spectrometer, which heats the sample then uses the light waves it emits to identify the substance, or used a reagent test if a drug in liquid form was presented.

The drug-checking industry was barely legal in New Zealand – it had passed through Parliament just a month earlier, making the service permanently legitimate and extending the temporary legislation rushed through 12 months earlier. 'It's about keeping people safe,' the Health Minister Andrew Little argued. Drug-checking services had intercepted potentially deadly substances in the community within the last year, and users often chose not to ingest their drugs once informed they weren't what they thought they'd bought.

For the first seven years that Know Your Stuff had worked at festivals, it was on the very edge of the law, the checking of illegal drugs was a grey area and their presence at events raising fears that organisers could be prosecuted for knowingly allowing drugs to be taken at their event. Understandably, some organisers simply refused to have Know Your Stuff at their events while other festival organisers pretended their events were drug-free. And in order to avoid prosecution themselves, the drug checkers made sure never to personally handle any of the drugs they were checking so they couldn't be charged with possession. As one researcher noted, drug checking was a daring and pioneering exercise.

While I was there that December evening in 2021, the results of more than 20 samples came back, and those who'd brought their drugs along for checking were nearly all in for good news. The one ketamine sample was ketamine, the three LSD trips that were tested were all LSD – but it wasn't that long ago that many people were bringing in what they thought was LSD only to find they'd bought a synthetic hallucinogen known as N-bomb (NBOMe), a very potent drug that has led to overdoses and deaths abroad. The rest of the drugs brought that night were all purported to be MDMA/ecstasy, in both pill and powder form, and nearly all of them were exactly that.

Of the two samples that weren't MDMA that night, one was known as mephedrone, referred to as 'MDMA's annoying younger cousin' by drug checkers. While it has a similar chemical structure to MDMA and many enjoy taking it, it doesn't recreate quite the same level of euphoria and can leave users feeling more strung out. And for the other poor fella, it turned out his pill was pure caffeine. He'd effectively just paid a lot of money for a very strong coffee.

There have been some other finds that may make you chuckle. The previous summer, they tested pills that contained only parexyl, a brand of toothpaste found in Europe; another contained nothing but plaster of Paris. Sucks if you bought this one, the testers said.

Know Your Stuff's deputy manager Dr Jez Weston told me that typically when people buy drugs within their community, they're much more likely to be getting what they paid for. It's at festivals where people might buy off strangers in the crowd that the risk of getting ripped off or buying dangerous substances grows. The previous summer, their team were regularly detecting supposed ecstasy pills that actually contained dangerous amounts of eutylone, a cathinone also known as bath salts. While eutylone initially creates feelings of euphoria and excitement, it's much more potent than ecstasy and takes a very, very long time to wear off, with some users suffering from hallucinations, psychosis and panic attacks. As Know Your Stuff's information pamphlet describes it: 'Eutylone: a shit time for a long time'.

Nearly a quarter of all MDMA samples they tested at festivals in the summer of 2020/2021 had eutylone in them, leading Know Your Stuff to coin it 'the summer of terrible drugs'. Some who took eutylone ended up not sleeping for two or three days, which is just not a fun way to party.

In a survey of drug users who had their substances checked by Know Your Stuff in the summer of 2020, 68 per cent indicated they'd modified their drug use because of the test results. Some took smaller amounts of the drug than they were originally planning to, about a third of them binned their drugs altogether when they realised they weren't what they'd thought they'd bought, and others avoided mixing their drugs with other substances after talking with drug checkers. And in her research into drug checking in New Zealand, Victoria University criminologist Dr Fiona Hutton also found that 90 per cent of those who had used Know Your Stuff's drug-checking service said their knowledge of how to keep safe when taking drugs had improved.

It's another initiative that appears to be delivering harm reduction in spades. Also, as the young Wellingtonians returned to the Drug Foundation's office after waiting 40 minutes for their drugs to be checked, each spoke with a volunteer about their results and got advice around harm reduction, often around dosage – 'that pill's really strong, perhaps break it in half'; 'hey, maybe only snort so much of this powder …'

I caught the lift back down to the street and chatted to one guy who'd had his drugs checked that evening. He said the test showed it was high-quality MDMA; he was stoked and clearly looking forward to consuming them. But as Jez Weston acknowledges, Know Your Stuff has spent much of its existence checking the drugs of predominantly wealthy white young people who are heading to festivals and raves, and as a result, the service seldom tests substances like methamphetamine or opiates. However, with drug checking's freshly legal status and an $800,000 injection of government funding, this is beginning to change. More spectrometers were purchased and they are now being loaned out to Needle Exchange centres and the New Zealand Prostitutes' Collective.

And while it is very early days, when I talked to the Drug Foundation's deputy executive director, Ben Birks Ang, in late 2022, they had tested nearly 50 samples of methamphetamine, with around 80 per cent of the samples pure methamphetamine, and those that weren't had been cut and bulked out with two main fillers, dimethyl sulfone, and the meth-lookalike isopropylbenzylamine. While neither pose great risk, users report they can be quite irritating if snorting their cut meth.

The drug testers have also noticed that while ecstasy and LSD users are often happy to sit and chat about their drug use and how to reduce harm, meth users appear to be a lot more stigmatised. They're a lot less keen to talk about harm-reduction strategies, and focused on getting out of there as fast as they can. They also want every last fleck of methamphetamine back so they can use it, Birks Ang told me.

Observing the Know Your Stuff event unfold, I couldn't shake the feeling that a most curious and contradictory system is now in place. Those participating in the drug-checking scheme face arrest if caught by police possessing these drugs when being purchased from their dealer or when travelling to their festival or party. Yet, at the same time they're being encouraged to have these same drugs tested in a legal, government-approved and funded programme to help keep them safe.

Go figure.

CHAPTER 12

THE 'MOST SNEAKIEST' DRUG IN THE WORLD

Community Helplines and Reaching the Unreachable

CHRISTINE REMUERA HAS NEVER PICKED UP A P PIPE IN HER life nor touched the drug herself, but she's had a hell of a lot more to do with methamphetamine than most of us. Ten of her immediate family members have been hooked on the drug, including her siblings, a few of her own kids and now some of her mokopuna, and she hasn't even counted her nieces and nephews. She's also had to help raise nine of her grandchildren because their parents' priority was P.

I'm sitting on a couch at the Wesley Community Action in Porirua in August 2021 with Christine, Rowena Wiki and Mike Hogan, three of the frontline workers with the methamphetamine support movement 'P' Pull, which helps people reclaim their lives from crystal meth and warns people about the pull that P has. For those who work at 'P' Pull, it's essential they have lived-experience with methamphetamine and can walk the talk, to ensure they're relatable to those seeking help. Between these three, they've had decades of experience of dealing with meth. And P Pull is just one of many organisations across the country that are trying to reduce the harm that meth is causing in their communities.

By her own admission, for years Christine Remuera had her head in the sand. She was pretending out of embarrassment that her family wasn't being ravaged by P, even in the face of intimidating visits from gang members looking for her kids and the money they were owed. Eventually, broken and traumatised from the stress and grief, Christine reached out to 'P' Pull for support; now she's the movement's national co-ordinator.

Mike Hogan is an addictions practitioner at the Taeaomanino Trust, a Pacific social service and health provider based in Porirua, and openly admits that for many years his own meth use was 'out the gate'; a self-described fun-junkie, he'd always been keen to party and spend a bit of cash. But the good times only lasted about two years because by then Mike had spent so much money on meth he'd sold his house and was selling meth solely to support his own habit. He couldn't get out of bed without taking a hit. Because he always knew where to score it, Mike also had a lot of friends who would pop over and buy some off him, but being a meth dealer, even a small-time pawn like he was, wasn't easy, he says.

So many of his clients would IOU their purchases, promising to pay for them later, that when his own dealer arrived he'd have to run around like a blue-arsed fly to find the money to pay for them. And being a meth dealer means you're up all hours, you're constantly sleep deprived, it was a mad crazy world he lived in. He says he once watched a mate stab his ceiling with a knife again and again, convinced someone was hiding up there watching him. Another heavy user he knew drew the attention and ire of neighbours when he began mowing his lawns at four in the morning.

'You become sort of clinically insane when you're hooked on meth,' he reckons. 'You're in another world, one where you withdraw and keep your distance from "normal people" who don't use the drug.'

By the time Mike managed to get into rehab he'd gone from owning a pretty successful second-hand shop in Porirua and having a bit of money to being broke, witnessing kidnappings and, on one occasion, having a gun held to his head.

Rowena Wiki's meth-addicted husband left her and her children to fend for themselves 17 years ago and for a long time she had no one to reach out to for help, everyone she knew was either using meth themselves or didn't understand her problem. Getting involved in 'P' Pull connected her with people who knew her language, knew what she'd been through, and allowed her to talk and grieve. It gave her a sense of community and Rowena says if it hadn't been for 'P' Pull, she's not sure where she'd be. Several of her adult children have followed in their father's footsteps and use meth now, and so she also has full-time care of three of her grandchildren.

The morning we chatted, Rowena had already hosted a Facebook Live for 'P' Pull's 8000 followers, focusing on whānau trauma and what steps people can take if they are having to raise other people's children or their own grandchildren because of someone's meth addiction – an incredibly common issue.

'P' Pull was launched by Liz Makalio and her husband and ex-user Dennis, a member of Porirua's Mongrel Mob Rogue chapter, in 2016, their vision to help communities across Aotearoa understand methamphetamine and help whānau and communities to stand up to the drug. Underlying the model is the Māori holistic health concept Te Whare Tapa Whā, which represents the four cornerstones of spiritual, physical, mental and whānau wellbeing.

The initiative began one Friday afternoon that year, when a young Porirua woman experiencing meth-induced psychosis walked into Wesley Community Action's Waitangirua centre seeking help. As the centre's manager, Liz Makalio called all the local drug and alcohol support services and the local hospital trying to find support for the woman, but there was simply none available. After taking the woman back to her own home for the weekend to detox, Liz tried again to find help the next week and came up short. Frustrated for these people experiencing P addiction, she created 'walk-in Mondays' where people could come and talk to someone face-to-face about what they are going through.

The walk-ins proved incredibly popular, particularly with families struggling with a meth addict and looking for advice or support. Seven years on, and 'P' Pull is now running 14 walk-ins across the central and lower North Island, including Taupō, Gisborne, Dannevirke, Murupara, Ruatoria, Levin and in multiple locations across Wellington. Their closed Facebook page is highly guarded; people are vetted to make sure they're there for legitimate reasons and not trying to score, and researchers and journalists have been banned from the site after 'P' Pull found they were approaching people for information and stories. Naturally 'P' Pull had felt this undermined both their clients' recovery and the movement's values of anonymity and compassion.

A week prior to this interview, 'P' Pull facilitators from around the country had hosted Facebook Lives where they shared their tips about self-care for whānau affected by meth. Christine told me for her it can be as little as giving herself a break – as easy as taking her socks off and walking outside on Papatūānuku (the land) or going to look at Tangaroa (the ocean), and chilling. A message they share time and again with whānau who are seeking support to deal with a loved one who is addicted to methamphetamine is for them to set healthy boundaries and not to become their enablers – don't lend them money and don't pay their rent or bills or buy their groceries because this only frees up their own money to buy more meth.

And that's not as easy as it sounds, Mike says. Family members can be driven crazy by the often highly manipulative meth user in their midst, but it's a parent's natural instinct to try to help their children. Christine says it took her years to realise she had to be cruel to be kind and to stop giving her kid money 'every blinkin' time they asked'.

But they're convinced New Zealand's meth problem is only getting worse. When he was using a decade ago, Mike was paying $1000 a gram. Now the people he helps who are hooked on it are buying it for $300–$400 a gram, it's just getting easier and cheaper to obtain. He's working with one client now who first tried meth when they were 12 and their old man gave them a hit.

In a 2019 television interview, Dennis Makalio described meth as evil and the 'most sneakiest' drug in the world, one that destroys everything in its path. Everyone he used to know and love who had used it simply aren't the same people anymore, he said.

For years, 'P' Pull got by on the smell of an oily rag, selling their 'Don't Meth Around' T-shirts and bumper stickers to raise money. Paying for the cups of tea and biscuits and scones they provided at their walk-ins out of their own pockets and stressing about whether they would have enough money to pay for the petrol needed to drive across town to their next meeting. That is until Wesley Community Action applied for a grant on behalf of the movement through the Proceeds of Crime Fund – a system that allows police to seize cash and assets that have been made through criminal endeavours and redistribute them to organisations and programmes trying to address crime or drug-related harm. It's funded everything from reintegration programmes for young women leaving prison, fog-cannons to deter robberies in dairies, and in 2020, 'P' Pull received $666,000 to continue its mahi for the next three years.

The funding has allowed more walk-ins to be held, and for more 'P' Pull facilitators to be trained and receive proper qualifications so they're better able to deal with the diverse range of issues that come to them, whether it be trauma support or counselling.

When I asked if they would change anything about the way we deal with methamphetamine in this country, Christine says there simply needs to be more support in place for the children and families of meth users. While the person addicted can go to rehab, there's a real lack of help available to those their use has affected. She'd also like to see more safe spaces so kids can get away from their parents if and when they're using.

Rowena says she wants to see more education in schools. Her two teenage daughters have been exposed to a lot of poor behaviour by their older siblings who use meth, and while she has tools she shares with her daughters to help them cope, she's worried about other kids growing up with meth addiction in their midst and where they can go to seek help.

With a decades-old cannabis conviction that stopped him from getting a job as a postie, Mike would like to see methamphetamine decriminalised. He says a conviction for any drug, especially a Class-A drug like meth, not only has a huge impact on your future potential in terms of work but also acts as a barrier to people getting well. 'They just go "fuck it, my life's shit and I'll never get a good job", but if you give people a second chance it can go a long way for those who are trying really hard to get well.'

One of "P' Pull's strengths, Mike tells me, is it has helped normalise talking about methamphetamine and addiction. He says that for a drug surrounded by huge stigma, that's an important first step. Another key part of their work is helping families develop their own action plans for managing a loved one on meth. They say as their work has gone on, they've learnt they're not just dealing with methamphetamine but all the interconnected issues of poverty, homelessness and hunger.

Nearly seven years after they launched, 'P' Pull estimates they're dealing with 600 whānau a week, throughout the North Island. Their promise is that they'll never ever turn a family in need away. 'We'll walk with them until we can find them the help they need.'

> When people ask me what do you tell people who want to try P, do you tell them it's bad? I tell them, nah it's good, it's that fucking good that you will do it again and again.
> Andrew Hopgood, counsellor and former P addict

If there's one thing that Liz and Dennis Makalio are insanely good at, says Andrew 'Hoppy' Hopgood, it's pulling in their community and reaching the unreachable. Hopgood is a recovered meth addict and now tutor and lecturer of counselling and addiction studies at the Wellington Institute of Technology. I'm sitting in Hoppy's kitchen with him, in his newly purchased home just off State Highway 2 between Featherston and Greytown.

A couple of weeks earlier, he'd caught my attention with his presentation at the Drug Foundation's symposium, 'Through the Maze: On the road to health'. The symposium had attracted an audience of hundreds to Parliament, a motley crew, with senior police officers and Corrections officials sitting alongside drug users and gang members, drug reform campaigners, the press and politicians, to talk about what's happening on the frontlines with drugs and rehab in New Zealand.

Hoppy told them that after 14 years of heavily abusing speed and then meth, he reached rock bottom in 2005. At 33 years old he was weighing in at just 49 kilograms, he was homeless, he didn't have any ID or a bank account, and he no longer had any fucking idea what normal was. Fast-forward 16 years, and

Hoppy's a qualified lecturer, a counsellor who works in rehabs and is also heavily involved in 'P' Pull. He reminded those at Parliament that while he and others work extensively with gang members trying to get off meth, they never ask them to leave their gangs behind – you need all the support you can get when you're trying to recover.

Now sitting in the Wairarapa, with his puppy snoring by our feet, Hoppy confesses that when he first received a phone call from Dennis Makalio asking how he was and if he would like to get involved in 'P' Pull, he nearly shat his pants. Having long being involved in a motorcycle gang himself where the golden rule, he said, was to stay the fuck away from the Mongrel Mob, here he was chatting to a member of its Porirua Rogue chapter and about to get involved in his anti-methamphetamine movement.

I asked Hoppy how he had ended up in the dire situation he'd told that crowd at Parliament about, a few weeks back, and he said for him it all started when he was adopted at just age three to a family in the Wellington suburb of Johnsonville. He didn't fit in, he didn't look like his adopted family and while they were big eaters, Hoppy didn't like food, so his adopted mum would end up force feeding him and threatening to send him back to the adoption agency. On occasion, she made him sit at the end of the driveway with his suitcase packed, told they were on the way to collect him.

With his adopted mum telling him his birth mother didn't want him, and that she didn't want him either, Hoppy's only weapon was food, which he used to fight back against his mum by refusing it. He regularly gave his school lunch away to his mates. One time a friend gave him a couple of cannabis joints in return, and those joints helped relieve the constant nausea from not eating. It changed Hoppy's outlook, if only temporarily, from angry to happy. And at around 17, he progressed to snorting speed and started to hang with 'a good bunch of likely lads' in a motorcycle club; the speed helped suppress his appetite and he was now eating around one small meal a day.

And it was in that motorcycle club, which I agreed not to name, that Hoppy finally found a sense of belonging. There was a lot of riding and a lot of partying and while he says he never saw anything too untoward, he says the gang also gave him status. If you needed drugs Hoppy could get them; if you needed firearms just ask. But gangs and drugs and firearms often draw the attention of law enforcement and it was a *bang, bang, bang* on the front door of his home in Waikanae at 6am when everything started turning pear-shaped.

Thinking it was a mate arriving, Hoppy opened the door only to find a cop standing there and he wasn't there to party. The officer promptly jammed his knee in the doorway as a freshly awoken, naked Hoppy tried to slam the door shut, his two-year-old pitbull latching on to the cop's leg. After getting the dog off the cop, he was allowed to put on his jeans and the police let him take his morning piss – and all the weed, cannabis oil, and a 'good eight or nine grams of speed' that were in his pockets flushed away with it.

It turned out to be part of a joint Police/Customs operation that hit more than 50 houses at once. Those arrested were locked up at prisons across Wellington, but it was kind of okay, Hoppy says. 'There were that many of us it was like being on holiday with the boys but just at a really fucking bad destination with shit food.' He ended up being charged with nine counts of conspiracy to supply amphetamines. After pleading guilty to some and having others dropped, he received a two-year suspended sentence and nine months periodic detention.

By his mid-twenties, he was having frequent, random nose bleeds as snorting so much speed had burnt a hole in his septum. Not much later when he arrived at a mate's workplace and was invited upstairs, he saw a bunch of crystals in a bowl. His mate placed some in a lightbulb and handed it over … and holy shit it was fucking good, he told me. Hoppy had just met P.

While the early 2000s are a bit of a blur for Hoppy, he says it was around then that he started using meth frequently and it wasn't long before P had him by the short and curlies. One thing he does recall is that in 2003, Tip Top bread bought out his pita bread franchise and he came into quite a lot of money and also now had an awful lot of spare time and his meth use went through the roof. And he wants to make it clear – he had a fucking ball – his life was one big fast-paced party. With meth came supreme confidence, energy and sociability. You just feel smarter, you're not doubting yourself, it's the perfect drug of abuse, he says, or to put it bluntly, 'You're a fucking predator.'

Because the drug is so good, it's part of the problem, he says, because the cracks don't really start to appear for a couple of years, by which time you and many of the people you know are using. Or as he said to those at the drug symposium at Parliament, 'Meth is fucking awesome until it isn't.'

With the money from the franchise sale and a whole lot of spare time to use meth, it was beginning to dawn on Hoppy that things were out of control. He and his girlfriend at the time had both repeatedly tried to get clean, but one would inevitably end up going out and scoring more meth from associates in the motorcycle gang and it would start all over again. He wasn't working, he wasn't eating, his life was on the skids, and she ended up running off with his best mate from high school.

But it was his daughter's birthday party, August 2005, where things truly fell apart. He arrived wearing leathers, on his Harley Davidson, and had been up for three days, then his daughter wouldn't let him into the house until he phoned his parents who hadn't heard from him in months and had no idea where he was. At the sound of his mum's voice he broke down in tears, as did his mum, while his daughter just looked at him like, 'What the fuck, Dad?' So he handed her over the birthday card he'd bought on the way to the party, wishing her a 'Happy 10th Birthday'. It was a white card with silver lettering – only to realise 'she was fucking 13'. And that was the exact moment, Hoppy told me, where he knew it all had to stop. He'd recently even been having suicidal thoughts and realised he was falling to bits. Looking back now, he thinks his daughter quite possibly saved his life.

At his wits' end, he called a friend who ran a dairy farm in Northland, who said he should come stay and get clean. He gathered up everything he owned in Wellington and put it into storage. Hoppy estimates he'd never really come down off drugs properly since the early 1990s and he'd certainly never got clean, but on the farm all there was to do was milk cows. He didn't have the option of using. And his mate had some blunt advice, saying, 'Maybe all you need to do is quit the gangsta shit and find out who you really were meant to be in the first place.'

Over the next two or three months in 2005 he weaned himself off meth and other drugs, came through the crazy depression and anxiety, and slowly his real personality and emotions began to come back, feelings he hadn't felt in 15 years – not anger or happiness but something in the middle. After a brief relapse in Wellington, Hoppy went up to the farm where, with a little serendipity, his mate's tattooist stopped by and offered him a job in a Wellington tattoo parlour. He'd get taught body piercing on the condition he stayed clean. So he ended working at Tattoo City in Cuba Mall, with a bunch of amazing colleagues who had also lived on the wild side and managed to get themselves clean. But Hoppy remembers there was one problem. He could barely have a conversation with someone if it wasn't about drugs, motorcycles or violence.

The work mates wrote him a list of conversation starters, a bunch of topics he could use with customers like what do you do for a living, have you got the day off work, mate, and they even had a bell they'd ring to let Hoppy know when his conversations had veered into the wildly inappropriate – 'One minute we're having a laugh, the next I'm the only one still laughing' – and when they rang that bell, he knew it was time to shut the fuck up.

One of his colleagues was into working out and gave Hoppy a training routine and help with his diet, and soon Hoppy had a sense of belonging and a sense of status, and while there were a few relapses over the next few years, the environment was warm and nurturing. From there, Hoppy started his own company, Tattoo New Zealand, in Mana where he did tattoo removals and fetish body piercings but he couldn't see a future in it; 'you kind of get sick of looking at vaginas and holding penises to be honest with you' he told me. But it did teach him bedside manners and about dealing with different cultures and sexualities and, importantly, not to judge. Hoppy reckons it helped set him up for counselling.

Which is why at 37 years old, off he went and enrolled in an addictions course at the Wellington Institute of Technology, where he learnt how to learn, how to write essays and he quickly found himself working in public and private rehab facilities and community programmes like 'P' Pull.

Not only is New Zealand woefully short on rehab facilities and clinicians, he reckons, but also it needs more diverse clinicians, to match the wide range of people using this drug – 'so we're not putting Mrs Doubtfire in front of Mr Gangsta anymore'. Being able to build rapport and relate to the drug user is critical for success. Another major beef Hoppy has with rehab is that so many of them are faith-based, when people who have been experiencing drug psychosis are often trying to shake off their old imaginary friends, the last thing they need is a new one rammed down their throats.

At Narcotics Anonymous, people are forced to admit they're addicts and helpless and powerless, all negative concepts when what people really need is positive, clinical, motivational interviewing, group work, exercise, nutrition and sleep. You might be an addict, but you're only an addict for now. You can take the power back. Getting clean is supposed to be exciting.

In Hoppy's eyes, addiction is the opposite of connection. What he'd really like to see is the widespread use of publicly funded Green Cards that counsellors could issue to those recovering from substance abuse to help them access public facilities like gyms, swimming pools, cooking classes; the simple things that will get people back into the community, talking with locals, something to help give them back their sense of belonging.

It is with a feeling of immense pride to Hoppy that his mum and dad got to see him clean up, get his degree and even be interviewed on television about drug addiction before they passed away. He reckons he regrets fuck-all, except the 15 years he wasn't there for his daughter, the 15 years where by his own admission he was a pretty shit dad.

And in Featherston, Hoppy's local community, meth use is still rampant, in fact he says it's bad throughout the Wairarapa, and he has also watched the price more than halve since the early 2000s. At the time of our interview he said it was going for around $400 a gram.

'Misplaced your meth?' one headline in the *Wairarapa Times-Age* recently read, the article revealing a couple of bags full of P, valued at hundreds of thousands of dollars had been found dropped on the streets in Carterton and had been handed in to the cops. The local police were inviting whoever had lost it to come down and collect it from the station. 'We may need to ask you some questions first, though.'

* * *

If addiction is the opposite of connection, as Hoppy says, then grassroots organisations like 'P' Pull are doing everything they can to be proactive in helping their local communities. But there's another peer-support group out there, that is as brave as its name.

CHAPTER 13

'HAVOC, HARM AND UPHEAVAL'
Support Networks and Fixing Lives

NICKY GOLDSBURY WAS SITTING AT HOME WATCHING THE breakfast show on tele when a story of a massive meth-lab blaze that had erupted during a police raid nearby in Katikati began to be reported. The registered nurse's casual interest turned to shock as she watched the footage of a large thickset guy with a Mongrel Mob tattoo across his chest being led away in handcuffs. This was because, although his face was blurred on the screen, she knew without a doubt that it was her son, Karl.

With the Armed Offenders Squad involved, Nicky knew it was going to be the worst-case scenario, she knew it was going to be shit; you've really done it this time, Karl, she thought to herself, you are really going to go away for a long, long time.

And she was right. Dubbed the kingpin of a meth-manufacturing operation by the local press, Karl received a sentence of just over ten years in prison with no chance of parole before five, but it wasn't really Karl, or herself in terms of her professional standing with her colleagues, that she felt sorry for. It was Karl's two teenage sons, both attending the local school, and with all the newspaper articles about their dad, every kid in town knew he was a mobster drug dealer, P addict and meth cook.

While Karl, nicknamed 'White Dog' by the mob, had regularly been in both trouble and prison before, including for methamphetamine offences, Nicky had taken him and his family into their home for 15 months while he was on electronic bail awaiting sentencing, just to remind him what it was like to be part of a family again. Nicky shared her story in a video interview published on the website of the methamphetamine family peer support group, Brave Hearts. When Karl served part of his sentence at Whanganui Prison, she took the opportunity to speak to a group of about 50 prisoners there, most of them gang members, about the effects that their behaviour has on their loved ones.

'We all serve your sentences with you,' she told them. 'We just do it in a different way. We especially miss you on special celebrations like at Christmas time, on birthdays and of course at the deaths of family members – all times when you should be there.'

She also knows the destruction that meth addiction can cause on families, and she said it made her feel sick to her stomach when she walked into her first Brave Hearts meeting at Tauranga Boys' College and saw around 60 mostly white, middle-aged people there, many who had kids struggling with meth addiction too. And she knew that part of the reason they were there was because of drug dealers like her son.

Nicky's story is just one of a handful of short, honest videos on the website giving accounts of the havoc, harm and upheaval that can come into a home when a family member is hooked on P. Another mum talks of taking out protection orders against her son; a dad talks of how P made his daughter a manipulative liar who would play her parents off against each another in order to get money to feed her habit; one parent thanks Brave Hearts for reinforcing to them that the most important thing they can possibly do is to look after themselves first, to ensure they survive and get through this.

Brave Hearts founder, Erin Scarlett O'Neill, told me when we met in a Tauranga cafe that theirs is the 'oxygen mask' principle: when the oxygen mask drops from above your aeroplane seat, make sure you put your own on first because, when there's chaos, you're no good to anyone if you can't breathe, you may as well just join them. After working with hundreds of families who have had loved ones using methamphetamine, O'Neill says people always have the same first instinct – they want to fix the addict – but that's the one thing they cannot do. They need to learn to stand back and get themselves into as strong a position as possible to cope with what is ahead.

For the last seven years, Erin O'Neill and her friend Rosalind Potter have run Brave Hearts together, after a chance meeting in Tauranga where they realised they were going through similarly traumatic experiences when one of their children had become hooked on meth. Erin's son was just 15 and at Sacred Heart College in Auckland, in the early 2000s, when a friend's mother let him try meth. By the following year he was using heavily – not that Erin knew at the time. His family just knew something was terribly wrong, so they sent him to psychologists and anger management courses and even on Outward Bound, but for a while he managed to hide it.

Yet, life at home was hell. He was punching holes in walls, he was stealing from Erin and had become a member of a South Auckland street gang the Killer Beez; in short, he was creating absolute mayhem. Erin lived in fear that his P dealers would arrive at the family home seeking overdue payments for drugs. In one media interview, she tells how he dragged the whole family into the dark world of crime and it reached the point where sometimes she wished he would die of an overdose to free him from the scourge. 'Meth isn't just evil,' she told the reporter of a local newspaper, 'it's a destroyer, a destroyer of everything.'

By age 19, her son had his first stint in rehab and the next ten years or so were spent in a hamster wheel of getting treatment, getting off meth, then promptly getting back on it. Eventually, though, with the help of a counsellor he respected, he got off the drug for good and managed to move on with his life. By this stage, Erin had moved to Tauranga to get away from Auckland, her son and the meth scene she'd unwillingly been dragged into. It was there at a business lunch that she met Rosalind, who told her about the battles she was having with one of her daughters who had also been addicted to P.

Desperate to know what else to do, Rosalind had sought help from the Tauranga police, and that's where Senior Constable Lindsay 'Red' Smith not only helped come up with a plan to help her – but said what was really needed was a support group for other families affected by meth addiction.

When Erin heard about this, Brave Hearts was born. They'd expected maybe five or ten people to turn up to their first meeting at Tauranga Boys' College, but when so many showed up, they knew meth was rife in the bay than they'd expected.

While every family is different, some parents have kids at home who are running amok, others are the grandparents, worried sick about their grandchildren and how to keep them safe when it's their mum or dad who might be using in their home, all of those who turned up or who turn to Brave Hearts are struggling with the stigma and stress of having a family member hooked on P.

Over time, Brave Hearts developed a whānau toolkit; a 10-point plan, under these broad headings:

1. accountability
2. consequences
3. monitor
4. check
5. abide by law
6. no benefit of the doubt
7. expect relapses
8. manage emotions
9. cease enabling
10. self-care

And, either in person, or during the pandemic over Zoom, Erin O'Neill has helped countless families write their own meth management plan, to help them focus on themselves and have a set of rules and guidelines they could follow.

The two most vital steps in the toolkit, she tells me, is to have clear consequences in place for the meth user, and the other is to cease enabling. That means not lending them money or buying them anything, no matter how sad a story they pitch, as more often than not that cash or those items are used to buy more meth.

In addition to helping families develop their plan or coping strategy, Brave Hearts runs monthly meetings and has a closed Facebook page with 2000 members where people share their journeys and get advice. After launching in Tauranga, the organisation has seen massive demand for their support group across the country.

On the day I met with O'Neill, Brave Hearts was holding support meetings in both Nelson and Manukau; the following day there was one taking place in Ōamaru, and they are now trying to train up enough volunteers to run meetings all across the country and bring in guest speakers. They know how needed this group and others like it are. Not long before, she and Rosalind had dealt with 100 enquiries from families desperately seeking support – in just one month. They're run off their feet. And it's just getting worse, she says. More and more people are seeking Brave Hearts' support all the time.

Brave Hearts survives financially on a smattering of lottery and local community grants, while local councils around the country sometimes chip in to help cover the costs of the meetings held in their communities. I ask Erin what she believes the government could be doing differently to help alleviate the harm caused by meth. More funding for addiction treatment, she says, and more support services like Brave Hearts are badly needed.

And one other thing, she tells me – the government should decriminalise the possession of methamphetamine. 'Meth users are just victims, too.'

This reminded me of something Professor Joe Boden had said when we were discussing the Christchurch Health and Development study and the effects of meth. He reported that while the vast majority of those who have used meth have never perpetrated or been the victim of violence, being a user did increase your odds of being involved in a violent incident. And part of that, Boden believes, could be attributed to the black-market nature of the meth trade.

As well as working on the study for 17 years, Boden was an advisor on the Labour government's expert panel in the run up to the referendum on legalising cannabis in 2020. The referendum was narrowly voted down, yet he said his personal view is that at the very least, no one should be penalised for being in possession of or consuming any substance. He described the way illegal drugs are classified in New Zealand as 'mind-boggling'.

Highly toxic drugs such as heroin sit alongside far less harmful drugs like psilocybin mushrooms and LSD as Class-A drugs, earning suppliers a potential life sentence. On the other hand, alcohol, another highly toxic and dangerous drug that causes immense harm is not only legal but its consumption is enthusiastically promoted – even glorified – and so many of our social events in this country revolve around its consumption. Our sporting legends have booze brands on their uniforms, liquor company logos are splashed over sports fields, it is advertised broadly on television and print, and our communities are full of brightly branded bottle stores offering an array of intoxicating specials. Boden believes it's about time New Zealand started using science to properly assess drugs' harm.

But, in 2009, when a top drug advisor to the British government wrote a research paper saying the way illegal drugs are handled by politicians is reminiscent of medieval debates about angels, it cost him his job.

Professor David Nutt, who was the chairman of the Advisory Council on the Misuse of Drugs, which makes recommendations to government on the control of harmful drugs, wrote that taking ecstasy was no riskier than riding a horse – with horse-riding accounting for around ten deaths and 100 road-accident fatalities in the UK a year. 'This attitude raises the critical question of why society tolerates – indeed encourages – certain forms of potentially harmful behaviour, but not others such as drug use,' he wrote.

He also argued alcohol and tobacco were way more dangerous than many illegal drugs including cannabis, LSD and ecstasy. While his analysis was well received by some organisations, who said it showed what drug policy might look like if it were based on research and evidence and not political and moral posturing, Professor Nutt was promptly sacked by the government. The Home Secretary said Nutt had damaged efforts to give the public clear messages about the dangers of drugs, and that the government remained determined to crack down on all illicit substances.

* * *

Another initiative Brave Hearts has been toying with would enable their volunteers to go into hospital and visit and cuddle the babies born to mothers who were using meth through their pregnancy – concerned the little ones would be going through painful detoxing and could do with some love. But science is proving that such babies don't appear to experience withdrawal symptoms, like newborns do with opioids, although neither do they appear to be quite as attentive as they should be and they seem to require a little more soothing and settling than other babies. And when it comes to their reflexes, well they're just a little bit uncoordinated.

These are the observations of University of Auckland Professor Trecia Wouldes who, for the last 15 or so years, has been following the lives and development of more than 100 Kiwi kids whose mums had used P to varying degrees while they were pregnant.

Methamphetamine was really starting to make headlines in New Zealand around 2002 when Wouldes was invited by colleagues at Brown University in the United States, together with researchers across four US cities, to become the fifth site to follow and track the lives of babies born to meth-using mums. She wasn't entirely keen to take part at first – she'd just been working on a study following children whose mums were in the methadone programme while pregnant, and she knew just how tough research like this can be. And the women's lives can be so chaotic it's hard to find enough willing to be involved in the research in the first place, let alone keeping them engaged in it over multiple years.

One of the reasons the US researchers wanted New Zealand to take part in the study is because in the US, babies are uplifted from their drug-using parents far more often than here – there 40 per cent of the babies in the study were removed from their parents by the time they were two, compared to only 13 per cent in Aotearoa, and most infants removed here are placed with their wider whānau.

That being said, in 2020, New Zealand's child protection agency, Oranga Tamariki, carried out a study into the role methamphetamine played in the removal of children less than 30 days old from their parents, and it found methamphetamine use was a factor in around half of all removals, with domestic violence a factor in almost two-thirds of uplifts.

With the number of women who are taking stimulants like methamphetamine rapidly growing globally, their impact on women of child-bearing age is a significant public health concern, and so Trecia Wouldes began recruiting pregnant women for the study.

Prenatal exposure to drugs can be a controversial field. In the mid-1980s, one small US study of '23 cocaine-using moms' set in motion a tidal wave of reporting in America that the use of cocaine, particularly crack-cocaine, during pregnancy could have catastrophic consequences on the children. Articles warned that a generation of delinquent, mostly black, brain-damaged crack babies, many with terrible deformities, were being born to their crack-addict mums who were clearly not fit to mother them: 'Cocaine claims its tiniest victims: Babies born addicted' was one such headline.

A column in *The Washington Post* in 1989 opened: 'The inner-city crack epidemic is now giving birth to the newest horror: a bio-underclass, a generation of physically damaged cocaine babies whose biological inferiority is stamped at birth.' And quoted an expert: 'This is permanent brain damage.

Whether it is 5 per cent or 15 per cent of the black community, it is there. And for those children, it is irrevocable.'

And on and on the scare-mongering reporting went: 'Cocaine babies, for example, have 15 times the risk of Sudden Infant Death Syndrome. But the dead babies may be the lucky ones. For some of the crack babies who survive, the first life experience is the agony of cocaine withdrawal. They suffer terribly.'

Fortunately for the kids, it was largely all shown to be bullshit. Most of the crack-baby claims that were made at the time were later disproved by well-designed studies, and concerns were also raised about the way in which the early crack-baby research was carried out. There was a noticeable lack of control groups, while other factors like alcohol, tobacco and other drug use weren't considered, nor crucially, was arguably the biggest factor in determining a child's future: poverty.

Soon, teachers were reporting they couldn't tell any difference between the so-called crack kids in their class and the others, while those children with obvious difficulties were shown to respond brilliantly to early interventions and intensive support.

A few years later, Dr Ira Chasnoff, whose original study of 23 babies was what had sparked the crack-baby furore, said his subsequent interactions with those children when they were a little older had revealed their development was actually pretty much normal, and they were really no different to other kids. Putting political correctness to one side, Dr Chasnoff said 'the crack babies were simply not the retarded imbeciles people talked about'. It turned out the dead babies weren't the lucky ones after all.

As for the 107 meth-using mums recruited into Trecia Wouldes' study, some of them stopped using methamphetamine as soon as they realised they were pregnant, others continued using P right the way through, and she believes about 15 of them still use P regularly to this day, more than 15 years on.

In the early days, Wouldes asked the women why they used P as opposed to other drugs, and many of them gave very similar answers: I can party all night and still get up in the morning and look after the kids, get off to work – and what a bonus, it keeps me slim too.

Just like when meth was legally prescribed here, it continues to be used as a pick-me-up and appetite suppressant by some women, and Wouldes agrees. 'It's a woman's drug,' she tells me in her university office across the road from Auckland Hospital, 'and it's a feel-good drug too. It gives you boundless energy, and it's an aphrodisiac, meaning sex on meth can be great.' The only problem was that many of the women found they became addicted to it.

Wouldes had recently been asked to work on a paper looking at meth and cocaine use by women around the world, and she said it was a real eye-opener just where meth is being used. For example, in Iran, she found a study showing 15 per cent of female sex workers there were using crystal meth, often together with opiates, to help them work longer hours and service more clients. Meanwhile, in Vietnam, female sex workers who were using meth said they saw it as stylish and higher class, and viewed it as less addictive than other drugs – but they also reported they engaged in riskier sexual behaviour, including unprotected sex with multiple partners while using meth.

Nearly every other drug is used overwhelmingly more by men, but with meth, there's now almost perfect global gender equality.

For Wouldes' study group of mothers, she said around half had been subjected to physical and sexual abuse before they started using meth, and many reported they were still being subjected regularly to domestic violence, and suffering from mental illness. The women were all living volatile lives. But despite a lot of them feeling their lives were chaotic and messy, the one thing they all had in common was that they were interested in the development of their children, they wanted to get them help if they needed it and they agreed to be part of her study.

The researchers in both the United States and Auckland followed up with the children at regular intervals as they aged, and they've noticed the children in their meth group have quite severe behavioural issues – or as Wouldes put it: 'These kids don't just have tantrums, they fly right off the Richter scale.' They're very impulsive and appear to have problems with their executive function – behaviour managed by the frontal cortex, or the 'air-traffic controller of your brain' and some have significant mental health issues too.

And when I asked her how much of this is down to the mother using meth, Wouldes said that's the $64,000 question, and she's not really too sure. Her US counterparts are convinced that all of the behavioural problems being demonstrated by these kids can be put down to their environment, not the meth. They believe the children's tumultuous upbringings – with parents who were often still using P heavily or abusing other substances, suffering from mental illness and growing up in homes ravaged by domestic violence, and of course, poverty – is what creates the problems.

But Trecia Wouldes isn't convinced that's right. She says even the parents who adopted some of the babies at birth and have raised them in good supportive homes with lots of resources have struggled with the child's behaviour. So, while school principals, the police and parents say these children have serious behavioural problems, nothing in their data shows it's linked to meth.

Early on, they did notice an impact on the motor skills and cognitive development of the boys only, at the age of three and four, where they couldn't balance as well as other children and they couldn't run as fluidly either. The study believes oestrogen may help protect the girls.

'It's unlikely any future All Blacks will emerge from this group,' Wouldes told a reporter investigating her findings. She also said that they were looking into whether alcohol could have played a part in affecting the children's development, as many of the mums who used meth during their pregnancy were also heavy drinkers.

But as statistically improbable as it would be in the first place, it's unlikely we'll ever know if one of these boys does go on to become an All Black because the study is now pretty much finished. Wouldes' colleagues in the US lost funding years ago and stopped tracking the kids, and while she ploughed on with cobbled-together research grants, she's just carrying out her final round of follow-ups with the Kiwi kids, who are now around 15. She says it's just too tough and too bleak to keep going.

She's turned her mind to something more positive: developing an interactive app for pregnant women, which could act as a brief intervention. Completely anonymously, mums-to-be could put information into the app about what substance, or substances, they were using and receive non-judgemental information and tips in return. As examples, if a pregnant woman can decrease their tobacco smoking, they can probably raise the weight of their baby by 300 grams; if they're going to smoke pot, the app might suggest that they express their milk before they do so. And depending on what information is put into the app, a referral to health services could also be made. Wouldes believes this new project might help her get over her frustration that mums-to-be aren't universally screened for drug use by midwives.

CHAPTER 14

THE PUNISHER

Wars on Drugs from Nixon to Duterte

IT TURNS OUT, WHEN GOVERNMENTS REFUSE TO REGULATE substances, they don't go away. They just come under the control of criminals. And it's the same story in drug markets all around the world. As writer Dan Baum put it, in a piece for *Harper's Magazine*:

> The desire for altered states of consciousness creates a market, and in suppressing that market we have created a class of genuine bad guys – pushers, gangbangers, smugglers, killers. Addiction is a hideous condition but it's rare. Most of what we hate and fear about drugs – the violence, the overdoses, the criminality – derives from prohibition, not the drugs.

When then Prime Minister Jacinda Ardern stood on the stage with other leaders from across the region at the East Asian Summit in Bangkok in 2019 for the obligatory, and often cringeworthy, family photo taken at such events, it was obvious that this one was going to be extra awkward. Because at this photo op she was sandwiched between Myanmar's leader, one-time democracy icon Aung San Suu Kyi, who now stood accused of ignoring grave human rights abuses in her country, and Philippines' notorious president, Rodrigo 'The Punisher' Duterte, who had endorsed a massacre of methamphetamine users in his country.

Duterte had urged police officers and even ordinary citizens to kill those who use crystal meth, which is known as 'shabu', promising that the fish in Manila Bay would grow fat feeding on their corpses. With this endorsement, police officers and vigilante death squads carried out thousands of extrajudicial killings of shabu users.

The vigilante death squads would follow the same modus operandi each time when carrying out a hit: they'd arrive in a team of four men, on two separate motorbikes with their licence plates removed. Wearing masks and motorcycle helmets to disguise their identity, one pair would block off the street to traffic while the other pair would enter the apartment of the suspected drug user, drag them into the street and execute them in cold blood, often in front of their horrified families and neighbours. The vigilantes, who had an uncanny knack of knowing exactly where drug users lived, were suspected of either being police officers themselves or at the very least were backed by them.

The Philippines' police force had a slightly different MO when it came to murdering drug users, however, police reports consistently claimed the clearly outnumbered suspect pulled a gun on police during an arrest forcing officers to fire. Shabu would always be found on the corpse. But their family and witnesses would say the suspect was unarmed and pleading for their life to be spared when they were gunned down. One report found shabu users seldom survived encounters with the police; they ended up dead 97 per cent of the time.

In one killing documented by photojournalists from Reuters news agency, a distraught young Filipino woman is held back by friends behind yellow police tape at the scene of her father's killing. Police had shot him dead at his home in Manila and then carried out his body in front of a crowd of family members and neighbours. In another photo, the bullet-ridden corpse of 17-year-old Ericka Fernandez lay in a Manila alley next to a barbie doll. Women and kids were not off limits.

One police officer told *The Guardian* newspaper that he had been personally involved in 'neutralising' 87 shabu users in 2016, and described how the shootings were carried out by ten highly trained special operation teams, each consisting of 16 officers. 'We're not bad policemen or homicidal maniacs,' he told the journalist, 'we're angels that God gave talent to, to get these bad souls back to heaven and cleanse them.'

And yet such a campaign of extrajudicial killings appears to have had almost no impact on the availability of meth, according to the country's drug tsar and former vice president, Leni Robredo, who said in 2020 it had dented shabu supply by about 1 per cent. Instead of chasing and gunning down drug peddlers on street corners, the Philippines police should be pursuing the big suppliers because they're the real enemy, she said, not the ordinary people.

Duterte fired her from the role a few days later.

The extrajudicial killings, carried out over several years, did attract some domestic protest, but the public perception in the Philippines is that shabu is exceptionally dangerous compared to other drugs and that many Filipinos were supportive of draconian measures.

Official estimates of how many people were killed in the crack-downs range wildly from around 6000 up to 20,000. Among those slaughtered were some of Duterte's political rivals whom he had added to his narco list. One mayor, who had promptly surrendered, was even gunned-down by police in what they claimed was a shoot-out in his prison cell; the CCTV footage of that incident was misplaced.

Yet reports of the massacres and death squads didn't stop then-Foreign Minister Murray McCully from hosting a meeting with President Duterte when Duterte spent a night in Auckland on his way home, after attending APEC in Peru in November 2016. The Punisher couldn't fly back to the Philippines via the United States because he had recently called President Barack Obama the son of a whore and told him to go to hell after Obama publicly condemned the killings.

A few months later, fishermen in Manila reported that the police were now ordering them to dump the bodies of the shabu users they'd killed out at sea, and said they'd often tie weights to their bodies to stop them floating up. True to the Punisher's word, fish were now growing fat on the corpses of drug users.

But the world's catastrophic war on drugs began long before Jacinda Ardern held The Punisher's hand.

* * *

It was the summer of '69 and while some were having the best days of their lives, the freshly elected US president Richard Nixon was facing problems on multiple fronts. Three hundred US troops a week were coming home in coffins from the increasingly unpopular Vietnam War that was dragging on without an end in sight, while many of the soldiers who did make it out alive were returning with a freshly formed heroin habit.

And it wasn't the only substance of concern. Federal agents were warning that drug use and abuse was at epidemic proportions across the country, and that on some university campuses, up to 60 per cent of students were now regular users of marijuana, much of it coming from Mexico.

For President Nixon, who'd vowed to be tough on crime during his election campaign and who personally despised drug use, something drastic had to be done. And that something was launching what at the time was the most profound and wide-ranging anti-drug campaign in US history. It began with Operation Intercept.

In September that year, with almost no prior warning, 2000 border and customs agents descended on Mexican border crossings in what was dubbed the biggest peace-time anti-narcotics search and destroy operation in US history. Soon, tens of thousands of cars and trucks and pedestrians were backed up, including 90,000 Americans who had gone to watch a bullfight in Tijuana, with motorists forced to sweat it out in stifling heat in queues as long as six hours, waiting their turn to be interrogated and have their vehicles searched. Those who looked dodgy or were uncooperative with authorities were often forced to strip naked.

Meanwhile, out in the Gulf of Mexico, the US coastguard and navy patrol boats were intercepting and searching small vessels, even boarding cruise ships to carry out their inspections.

Back home, news of Operation Intercept made the papers, with *The Press* reporting on the interception of a small plane with nearly half a tonne of marijuana on board. The rented aircraft had tried to evade US authorities but was forced to land at an airport in Bakersfield, California, and after being captured, the 23-year-old pilot, Michael Mitchell, confessed he'd paid Mexican growers US$24,000 for the haul. The university student had actually been caught before Operation Intercept officially began, but the announcement of the seizure was delayed so it coincided with the crackdown.

Operation Intercept was causing so much chaos at the borders, and infuriating millions of people trying to cross, that vehicle searches were significantly scaled back after just ten days and removed altogether after 20. But while it copped considerable criticism and damaged diplomatic relations, it also generated a huge amount of tough-on-crime publicity for President Nixon. Mexico signed an agreement with the US called Operation Cooperation around the same time, agreeing to do more to combat marijuana production on its own turf.

To combat heroin, Nixon even dispatched a White House aide to Türkay with a blank cheque, hoping to convince their government to buy up their nation's entire opium crop and burn it. But Türkay baulked at that idea. Not only was growing opium legal in their country but also as one of their officials at the time put it, how could the Turkish government reasonably expect their 70,000 poor opium farmers to give up part of their income because rich Americans couldn't keep their noses clean. Türkay did, however, accept US$3 million from them to beef up its narcotics police so they could better monitor the illegal diversion of opium to smugglers.

Under Nixon's watch, combatting hard drugs became a key part of US foreign policy, America making it an agenda item at the United Nations and NATO.

And nearly two years after the agents had descended on the Mexican border, President Nixon, speaking from the White House in June 1971, delivered these words to the US press: 'Public enemy number one in the United States is drug abuse. In order to fight and defeat this enemy it is necessary to wage a new all-out offensive.'

Somewhat ironically, Nixon's announcement that day was actually focused on new funding of US$155 million for heroin rehab, research and education, nevertheless it's gone down in history as the official start of the 50-year-long war on drugs. It kicked off a massive increase in global law enforcement and punishments for those who produced, sold and consumed drugs, in the hope of creating a utopia. A drug-free world.

* * *

Five decades on and what we've got resembles a bloodbath more than a dreamland.

In addition to the vast numbers of drug users and civilians who have been slaughtered in drug-related conflicts over the last 50 years, tens of millions of drug users, farmers, couriers and small-time dealers have been locked up across the planet. And here's the kicker: it hasn't had any impact whatsoever in terms of reducing the availability of illicit drugs. Actually, the opposite is true – the size of the world's illegal drug market has simply ballooned.

The UN Office on Drugs and Crime said that cocaine production was at record levels in 2022; the amount of methamphetamine being cooked around the planet is skyrocketing year on year. Tens of millions of people use drugs like methamphetamine, while several hundred million adults use cannabis – between 5 and 6 per cent of adults around the world are taking an illegal drug every year and the numbers are rising.

According to the Global Commission on Drug Policy, these facts illustrate just what a complete and utter abject failure the war on drugs has been. Because, no matter how many people you arrest and incarcerate, their 2011 War on Drugs report argued, there's no shortage of people who will engage in such activity in order to escape poverty.

The commission is a think-tank of world leaders and personalities, including the likes of former UN Secretary-General Kofi Annan, Sir Richard Branson, and is presently led by our own former prime minister, Helen Clark. It is urging governments to abandon the war on drugs and decriminalise their use, warning that not to do so is both naive and dangerous. Naive because prohibition has had almost no effect on drug use, and dangerous, because drug laws alienate otherwise law-abiding people from the state, they divert police from targeting serious criminal networks and they fuel human-rights abuses and contribute to the drug-related deaths of an estimated 200,000 people each year.

The commission wants criminal penalties for drug use removed and replaced with administrative punishments such as fines, preferably fines accompanied by medical treatment and social support. It has also made a plea to world leaders to break the taboo surrounding drugs, to take a stand on the issue, to have the courage to say publicly what they privately know to be true, that a war on drugs can never be won.

This was one of Colombian President Gustavo Petro's first moves when he was elected in 2022. At his inauguration celebration in Bogota he said it was time that people accepted that the war on drugs had been a complete failure and he was going to legalise cannabis.

Colombians know a lot more about that war than most. Over the last 20 years the United States provided the country with NZ$13 billion in military aid to wage its own internal war against the rebel groups, cartels and narco-traffickers, farmers and whole villages involved in the cocaine trade. The brutal war has cost vast numbers of Colombians their lives, many of them civilians. And as for the cocaine?

In 2021, Colombian farmers planted 204,000 hectares of coca, a massive 40 per cent increase on the year before, the biggest crop since the UN Office on Drugs and Crime began monitoring the country's cocaine production more than two decades prior. Colombian cocaine exports soared too, with 1400 tonnes of cocaine sent mostly to Europe and North America that year.

As one of the government's new senators, Gustavo Bolivar told CNN, Colombia would never achieve peace until it regulated drugs. 'Right now, Colombia produces more drugs than when Pablo Escobar was alive, there are more consumers, more farmers. The drug trade is growing despite the money we invest in fighting it, and the thousands of deaths we suffer.'

* * *

On the fiftieth anniversary of President Nixon's war on drugs announcement, the NZ Drug Foundation released a video highlighting the toll such a war had taken in New Zealand. It reported that more than 50,000 New Zealanders had received a drug conviction in the last ten years, while hundreds of millions of taxpayers' dollars had been spent prosecuting those offenders. In 2020 alone, 850 Kiwi adults were imprisoned for low-level drug offences.

The New Zealand government has pulled just about every lever it could to try and win the fight against P, since the early 2000s. Defences have been boosted at the border, police force numbers bolstered, the cold and flu medications that contain the precursor pseudoephedrine were banned from pharmacies, while more than 2000 meth labs and their cooks have been taken down.

Counter-methamphetamine intelligence has been invested in, both here and overseas, even stationing Customs officials in Asia to combat the meth trade. Twenty years ago, methamphetamine was reclassified as a Class-A drug, bringing in the maximum possible punishments for those using and supplying P. Every year, several thousand New Zealanders are brought before the courts on such charges, and thousands of people have been incarcerated.

The NZ Drug Foundation reckons we're spending around $280 million a year on law enforcement when it comes to drugs, around four times more than is spent on treatment programmes to help those who are dependent on them. And yet the price of methamphetamine has collapsed. It's now much cheaper to purchase the drug, whether you're a P fan looking to hook up a gram, or an importer or dealer who trades by the kilo. Those who use P report it's as easy to get as it has ever been – for several years now, it's apparently been easier to get meth in parts of the country than cannabis.

In the year 1993, New Zealand border agents intercepted just under one kilo of methamphetamine in 16 small parcels. Three decades on, police and Customs are regularly busting shipments and stashes in the hundreds of kilos, while the amount of meth detected in our wastewater hit unprecedented levels in 2022.

Our law enforcement heavy-approach to methamphetamine doesn't appear to have had any impact on reducing supply; there's more P arriving here now than there's ever been. And while we may not have reduced the availability of P, our blackmarket for meth has generated incredible profits and wealth for those prepared to risk supplying the drug, while there's no shortage of criminal groups looking to cash in.

It's part of a global phenomenon and a widely acknowledged side-effect of the war on drugs, as even those tasked with leading the battle acknowledge:

> Over time, international controls have limited the number of people who take illicit drugs to a small fraction of the world's adult population, much smaller than those who use other addictive substances, like tobacco and alcohol. This undeniable success has also had a dramatic unintended consequence: a criminal market of staggering proportions.
> UN Office on Drugs and Crime, 2008

Dressed casually in Under Armour shorts, blue sneakers and a singlet emblazoned with the logo of his Phuket-based supplements company, Nutrition Depot, the stocky foreigner was making his way to do some shopping at a mall in Lat Krabang district in Bangkok. But, watching him was a squad of local police officers from the crime suppression division. It was 19 October 2022.

The businessman had entered Thailand on a short-term tourist visa a few years earlier and just hadn't got around to ever leaving, instead setting up multiple companies – a gym, a supplement store, a tattoo parlour and a restaurant – with his Thai wife in Phuket. But it wasn't the visa overstayer breach that had piqued the police's interest. This 43-year-old New Zealander was wanted by the FBI. After being given the green light to make the arrest, the Thai police officers swooped in and nabbed him: Shane Ngakuru, a gangster accused by authorities of being a 'super facilitator', working closely with Asian drug syndicates to orchestrate huge shipments of methamphetamine to New Zealand.

The wheels of justice turned quickly in Bangkok. By the following day, balaclava-clad assault-weapon-carrying police commandos had delivered Ngakuru to the airport for his one-way flight to the United States, to face charges of racketeering, and potentially spend the rest of his life behind bars.

A few months later, in January 2023, Turkish police officers from the Fight Against Organized Crime department carried out a surprise raid of their own on an address in the Zekeriyaköy neighbourhood of Istanbul and arrested Duax Hohepa Ngakuru, Australia's most-wanted man and the supreme commander of the Comanchero outlaw motorcycle gang. These two Kiwi cousins who made it big on the international stage in their chosen field, have been hunted down by law enforcement across the planet, authorities who accuse Duax and Shane Ngakura of being bonafide drug lords.

Duax was born in Rotorua in 1979 but grew up in Sydney and rose to the top of the Comancheros, before moving to Türkay in 2010, where he is accused of being the brains behind a $100-million-dollar drug empire. While he made a habit of keeping a low profile, a rare photo of him had recently emerged, chilling on a super-yacht in Türkay.

By all appearances Duax Ngakura was living the high life. But the net began closing in on the Ngakura cousins after they fell victim to an elaborate online scam, along with thousands of other criminals around the world, once they began using the messaging app ANOM. It was marketed to the criminal underworld as an impenetrable encrypted platform, one on which they could communicate in complete confidence, their conversations unable to be intercepted by law enforcement.

Unfortunately for ANOM users, the app was controlled by the FBI and every message they'd sent via the app was now evidence against them. Around 500 ANOM users found this out the hard way when they were arrested in a worldwide two-day takedown by police in June 2021.

In celebrating the sting, acting US Attorney-General Randy Grossman noted that encrypted devices normally provide criminals a valuable shield from law enforcement. 'The supreme irony here is that the very devices these criminals were using to hide from law enforcement were actually beacons for law enforcement.'

The aptly named Operation Trojan Shield resulted in the seizure of more than eight tonnes of cocaine, 22 tonnes of marijuana, two tonnes of meth, six tonnes of precursor chemicals, several hundred firearms and more than $48 million in different currencies, while 50 drug labs were busted. Part of the beauty of the operation, from law enforcement's point of view, was that the ANOM devices had been enthusiastically distributed by the criminal networks themselves, including by Shane Ngakura, who was promptly indicted in the US, along with 16 other foreigners, on charges of racketeering. He stands accused of belonging to a criminal enterprise that was laundering money, trafficking drugs and obstructing justice.

In New Zealand, police held their own press conference highlighting their role in Operation Trojan Shield, and several other related operations executed at the same time. They'd deployed more than 300 officers, including their national organised-crime team, the armed offenders squad, the special tactics group, their high-tech crime team and their cash-sniffing dogs as they issued 37 search warrants across the North Island and arrested 35 people, including senior members of the Waikato Comancheros, the Waikato Mongrel Mob and the Head Hunters.

And while the police restrained a few million dollars in assets that day, seized some cash, a bit of meth, a few kilos of the precursor iodine and 'some large bags of cannabis', they also disclosed a longer-running investigation, Operation Van.

For several years, the police had worked with Customs and the Government Communications Security Bureau, along with the FBI and Australian Federal Police, and had identified how meth and cocaine were being trafficked here by the Comancheros, namely by Duax Ngakuru. A few months later, *The New Zealand Herald*'s crime reporter Jared Savage revealed that as a result of Operation Van, more than 40 people were facing 1200 charges, and he published some of the police accusations relating to those cases.

The police alleged Duax Ngakuru had extensive ties to Mexican cartels and drug syndicates in China and the Middle East, that he had employed a number of ingenious methods to smuggle in tens of millions of dollars of meth and cocaine into the country, and that he boasted of having a suite of corrupt port, airport and postal workers at the ready. One of those arrested in connection with Operation Van was Lionel McDonald, who was caught in 2019 with nearly 140 kilos of methamphetamine disguised as bags of Chinese tea.

Savage also revealed that the police had recently laid a host of charges against Duax Ngakuru – drug conspiracy, importation and supply offences, money laundering and participation in an organised criminal group. They wanted him extradited from Türkay to face the music back home. In early 2023, that looked very much on the cards.

* * *

Gangsters and the underworld have clearly seized the day when it comes to controlling the importation and distribution of methamphetamine in Aotearoa, earning themselves enormous profits and wealth, and occasionally lengthy prison sentences, in the process. But as history has shown again and again, when you ban substances like alcohol or cocaine or methamphetamine, all you're really doing is handing over their control to criminal groups who bring with them an incredible tendency to deploy violence. These following case studies are just a few high-profile examples of the horrendous violence and mayhem that surrounds the methamphetamine market here in New Zealand, but they illustrate that when your most dangerous individuals and organisations control the distribution of a highly sought-after and powerful drug, it is a recipe for maximum harm.

So, when a naked and bound man threw himself out of a moving vehicle and ran straight into oncoming traffic in order to escape his captors in New Lynn in November 2019, one of the most disturbing examples of how disputes are dealt with in the meth world came to light. Twelve hours earlier, the man, who was referred to as Mr D in court, had been lured to a house in New Lynn by a group of Bloods gang members and meth addicts, who believed Mr D had robbed someone else of thousands of dollars. They were determined to recover the cash.

As Mr D entered, he was set upon, hogtied, stripped, kicked and beaten, they stole his wallet and keys, urinated on him and threatened to cut off his dick, they repeatedly demanded Mr D hand over the stolen money even though he repeatedly told them he had no idea where it was. In what a judge later described as something akin to a scene in a Quentin Tarantino movie, throughout the day five gang members took turns inflicting horrific injuries on him. They placed a cutdown .22 rifle to the back of his head and threatened to execute him, they shot him through both feet and used a blow torch to burn his feet, legs, stomach and back. They cut his pinky finger off with a pair of secateurs, sprayed liquid in his eyes and beat him around the head with a metal bar.

After hours of torture, and having been moved between addresses, the gangsters put Mr D in the rear footwell of his car, tying his hands with rope and his eyes with tape. They began driving him towards Piha where Mr D believed, perhaps not unreasonably, they would burn him alive. While driving along Fruitvale Road in New Lynn, Mr D managed to untie the rope and climb into the front seat where he lunged at the driver's face and leapt out the passenger's side door, to be rescued by a passing motorist.

In his victim impact statement, Mr D told the court his attackers were 'mentally ill, pathetic meth heads'. He said if he hadn't saved his own life by jumping from his own car he would have been burned alive and that every morning now he wakes up and looks at his scars and missing finger. As some of his five attackers were jailed, Mr D's mum spoke in court about the traumatic injuries her son suffered, his fractured skull, the burns and how she couldn't recognise him when she first saw him at the hospital. His father said he'll ever forget seeing his son's head so beaten and swollen it was twice its normal size.

But this wasn't the end of the ordeal. A month after Mr D escaped his torturers, the police warned the family a contract had been placed on their son and a hitman was coming for him. The family had to flee their house and eventually they escaped with their still-badly-wounded son overseas to safety.

A few years earlier, motorists stopped at the lights on Huia Road in Papatoetoe, Auckland, were startled when a slightly built woman appeared to fall out of the boot of a silver sedan in front of them and land heavily on the road. As they jumped out of their cars to help the woman, they noticed her ankles were duct-taped, she'd been tied with ropes and she'd clearly just hit her head badly on the road. They put her in the recovery position, but she was frothing at the mouth and making gurgling noises.

The 50-year-old Thai woman, Jindarat Prutsiriporn, known as Nui, had been kidnapped 22 hours earlier by a group of Head Hunters known as the Ghost Unit, who in turn had been hired by a 27-year-old Cambodian man who had fallen out with Nui over money and meth. She was heavily involved in the meth world, and had been imprisoned previously for importing and supplying the drug. Luring her from her home under the pretence of a meth deal, the Ghost Unit snatched her and drove her around Auckland in the back seat and boot of various cars for the best part of a day, threatening to shoot her if she screamed or hurt her family if she tried anything.

At one point when Nui was held in a garage, she managed to obtain a chef's steel that she hid on her and later used it to force the lock and open the boot of the sedan at that Papatoetoe intersection. But unlike Mr D, hers wasn't a lucky escape. Nui died in hospital two days later from head injuries sustained as she fell from the car, trying to escape her captors.

As for the entrepreneurial Ngakura cousins, they may stand accused of orchestrating huge meth shipments to New Zealand but it's their Commanchero mates on the ground in Aotearoa who help distribute it. And their willingness to dish out ruthless violence was on full display when they carried out an execution near Auckland Airport in 2018.

A passing motorist called emergency services at around 6 am after they saw what they thought were two bodies on Greenwood Drive in Māngere. When police arrived, they found 28-year-old Epalahame Tu'uheava dead at the scene, he'd been shot seven times, while his wife Mele had been shot twice in the head but was still breathing; she'd survived by playing dead.

The couple had gone to Greenwood Drive to conduct a meth deal, but the Comancheros proceeded to order them out of their car and shot them instead. As one of the gangsters later told the cops, Epalahame Tu'uheava was making money off the Comancheros' name so they decided to 'put him to sleep'.

During their trial, Mele Tu'uheava told the court she knew her husband was up to something dodgy when she found tens of thousands of dollars in their luggage as they returned from a trip to Invercargill. They'd recently returned from Australia where he had been a patched member of the Nomads, but when they got home he'd started to take a shine to the Comancheros. He'd sit watching their social media videos where they showed off their wealth and motorbikes and reached out to them.

It turned out to be a fatal attraction. As the police officer in charge of the case told the press following the sentencing of two of the offenders, Tu'uheava's son was now growing up without his father; every day he'd look at pictures of him and wear his clothes. Mele Tu'uheava was left with life-long injuries.

If, as has been shown, leaving the regulation of drugs up to hardened criminals leads to such disastrous results, perhaps the fact that more and more countries are starting to change tack will bring about necessary change.

Some governments are removing penalties for drug possession and pointing the users in the direction of healthcare and addiction treatment. Others have adopted safe-supply schemes, even for meth, where drug addicts are given the illegal substances they're dependent on, taking drugs out of the black-market and into safe, regulated spaces.

In New Zealand, the question is: do we follow suit?

CHAPTER 15

FRANKENSTEIN: BREAKING THE CYCLE

Making Addiction a Health Issue

AS THE METH USER OPENS THEIR FRONT DOOR, THEY REALISE that it's a plainclothes police officer who's come knocking. Their details have come to the police's attention after they took down a P dealer and searched their phone contacts.

But the cop isn't there to arrest the man, instead he's letting him know he can have a referral to the methamphetamine treatment programme, Te Ara Oranga.

'What is the benefit of prosecuting them?' the police officer asks. 'Aren't we better off trying to help them get off the drug ... and help them turn their life around?'

Detective Sergeant Shane Gilmer is talking to RNZ journalist Guyon Espiner, and the scene above was a re-enactment of a typical Te Ara Oranga intervention, for Espiner's 2022 documentary *Wasted*, which analyses why the world appears to be passing New Zealand by in changing its approach to drug use.

While Aotearoa still prosecutes thousands of people for using drugs every year, other countries are moving to legalise and decriminalise drugs, believing it is time to adopt a health-based approach.

Te Ara Oranga, The Path to Wellbeing, is New Zealand's exception to the rule. Launched in 2016, the Northland programme is considered by many to be a game changer, it's brought together police, health services, iwi and local support services, a total wrap-around community effort to show people hooked on P that there's an alternative to a life of gangs and meth. In the last few years it's helped more 3000 meth users and their whānau by providing culturally appropriate, community-led treatment in the form of a 16-week programme, which has reduced reoffending by 34 per cent and for every dollar spent on the programme, it delivers a return of up to seven bucks.

It's been such a success in Northland that it's now been rolled out in the Bay of Plenty, and in June 2022, then Health Minister Andrew Little announced the first services were up and running in Murupara. Not only does the programme get people off meth, he said, but it also got them back into employment, it brought them back together with their whānau, and reduced family violence and other crimes.

What's not to like? NZ Drug Foundation believes Te Ara Oranga could be rolled out across the country for less than $50 million and would deliver a return on investment of around $150 million.

What is interesting is that the police officers involved with Te Ara Oranga are effectively running a decriminalisation experiment in Northland, where rather than putting meth users in handcuffs they're directing them towards help, while at the same time still targeting and taking down dealers.

And although it's small in scale, it has already delivered some incredible results.

But across the Tasman they're moving much faster.

When she announced that the Australian Capital Territory would be decriminalising the possession of drugs like cocaine, ecstasy and ice, the state's health boss, Rachel Stephen-Smith, said it was abundantly clear that drug laws don't work. 'We know from research and evidence around the world that criminalising drug users does not reduce drug use and that treating drug addiction as a health issue improves outcomes for everyone in the community,' she said in 2022.

She said polls had shown that Canberrans overwhelmingly support drug decriminalisation.

Meanwhile, also in 2022, the New South Wales state government injected half a billion dollars into rehab services and justice initiatives aimed at helping get Aussies off ice. Over the next four years, $360 million would be pumped into health-related programmes, boosting the availability of evidence-based treatment programmes and early-intervention initiatives particularly in rural communities and regional NSW. They were hoping to reach and support an additional 11,000 Australians who use ice and promised a special focus on their 'priority populations', including youth, those with mental illness, Aboriginal people and pregnant women.

The state's deputy premier, Paul Toole, said, 'Every family in New South Wales who was grappling with a loved one's addiction would now know they'd be able to access the services they need to help break the cycle.' Another $140 million would go to ice-related justice initiatives, there would be more money for their drug courts, youth courts and more opportunities to refer addicts into treatment programmes.

And while New South Wales politicians were adamant they weren't going soft on drugs and were not decriminalising methamphetamine, they did introduce a pre-court diversion scheme for people caught possessing ice. It now meant that anyone busted using meth would effectively get a fine or a ticket from the police, with the fine waived if the offender accessed a drug and alcohol support service. Effectively it's a two-strikes policy – you get two chances – and if you're unlucky enough to get caught a third time, it's off to court you go.

If to some New Zealanders this might sound like a radical move, experts advised our government to do something similar more than ten years ago. In 2010, the Law Commission released its review of our Misuse of Drugs Act and argued it was time we took a more proportionate approach to policing drugs. We are criminalising thousands of people whose drug use is causing no harm to others, the Law Commission argued, and in some cases that drug use is linked to underlying health issues like drug dependence and mental illness.

The Law Commission's president, former prime minister Sir Geoffrey Palmer, recommended that we introduce a mandatory cautioning system for people caught possessing drugs. The number of cautions you'd be allowed would vary depending on which drug you got busted with. Someone caught with a Class-A drug like P would have to attend a brief health-based intervention on their first caution; someone nabbed with a Class-B drug like ecstasy would have to attend an intervention following their second caution; someone sprung with a little Class-C weed would get three cautions.

But there would be a limit to the cautioning system's patience; the possession of drugs remained a criminal offence and anyone busted again after receiving their final caution would be prosecuted.

For some users, a caution would be a get-out-of-jail-free card, for others it would mean they could escape the life-altering consequences of a criminal conviction.

Also under the Law Commission's proposed scheme, the police would have distributed information on the potential health and legal impacts of using drugs as well as the contact details of treatment services, while issuing cautions. The beauty of the cautioning scheme, Palmer explained, was that it would free up the criminal justice system from dealing with minor drug offences, while providing greater access to healthcare for those needing treatment. And while he acknowledged the police already had discretion not to prosecute people, Palmer said the problem was that discretion leads to discrimination, and it was already abundantly clear that police are biased against certain types of people, like Māori, when deciding who to prosecute. That's diplomatic speak for they're racist yo.

However, it would be fair to say that Palmer's recommendations weren't greeted with open arms by John Key's National Government; rather they were publicly jeered. Justice Minister Simon Power vowed he would never show drug users more leniency. The anti-drug warrior said his boss John Key had declared a war on P and if the government softened its approach on meth users in any way, they would only be undermining that war.

Nearly 15 years later and these politicians are just photos on the walls at Parliament and meth's foothold remains undiminished – if anything, gangs have greater control over the importation and distribution of meth now than when those politicians were vowing to take them down.

In 2018, the Labour Government ordered an official inquiry into mental health and addiction, He Ara Oranga, which recommended that the government decriminalise drugs. He Ara Oranga found the criminalisation of drugs creates a barrier for those in need of help, while a conviction for personal drug-use has far-reaching impacts on people's lives. 'Criminal sanctions for the possession for personal use of controlled drugs should be replaced with civil responses, such as fines or treatment programmes,' they announced.

While Labour did tweak the Misuse of Drugs Act the following year to encourage police to use their discretion and refer drug users to treatment rather than prosecuting them, they have refused to go further, citing the 2020 cannabis referendum defeat, and the police are still opting to prosecute thousands of people for low-level drug-possession offences.

But there appears to be decent public support for decriminalisation in New Zealand – in fact it's two-to-one. In 2022, 1000 Kiwi adults were polled and asked if New Zealand should decriminalise the possession of small amounts of illegal drugs, and instead refer drug users to health services? Sixty-one per cent were on board with that idea, 30 per cent were against and the rest didn't know.

Other countries aren't mucking around. British Columbia has decriminalised the possession of drugs and as of early 2023, any resident there can have up to 2.5 grams of ecstasy, meth, heroin or cocaine on them without fear of arrest. In fact, now if you do come to the attention of the cops while carrying drugs, they're not even allowed to confiscate them, but they will hand out health referral cards, gently encouraging users to seek treatment.

The provincial government of British Columbia said the decriminalisation of drugs is a critical step in the fight against overdose deaths and one that would knock down the barriers and stigma that stops people from accessing life-saving support and treatment. 'Substance use is a public health matter, not a criminal justice issue,' it stated.

The move to decriminalise is part of the province's response to the opioid crisis in North America, where drugs laced with fentanyl have killed hundreds of thousands of people including 33,000 Canadians since 2016. About a third of those deaths have happened in and around Vancouver, where drug overdoses are now the leading cause of death for those aged between 20 and 40.

The Canadian government, in trying to stop the carnage, has rolled out multiple safer-supply programmes across the country, where drug users can obtain non-tainted government-issued opioids.

A survey of drug users who accessed safer-supply programmes found their use of street drugs decreased, as did the number of overdoses, while some participants reported that being in the programme was life-changing. Not having to spend their time hunting down their drugs on the street made them more productive, constructive and positive. One user said the safer-supply programme had 'enabled me to move forward in my life and not be at a standstill'; another said they were '100 per cent more stable than I have ever been.'

Similar schemes are now in place in other countries where they've faced crises with drugs.

In Switzerland in the 1980s and 90s, there was an escalation in the number of people using heroin and those people contracting HIV from sharing needles. And so in 1992, a heroin-assisted treatment programme was introduced, where users were given medical-grade heroin.

There was a catch – you had to use it in a clinic, which you could attend up to three times a day – but it meant users were getting unadulterated drugs and were using clean equipment and weren't overdosing. Over time, those in the programme began using less heroin, their health improved and because they were only paying a token fee to get their hit, they committed less crime because they didn't need to steal any more to support their habit.

Could a programme like this work for methamphetamine in New Zealand?

Well, in 2022, NZ Drug Foundation together with The Helen Clark Foundation (an independent, non-partisan public policy think-tank) released a report into meth that suggested maybe it's about time we gave more proactive methods a shot. They called for trials to be run where those who are heavily dependent on methamphetamine could receive a monitored daily dose of a similar stimulant, like dextroamphetamine or Ritalin, or even methamphetamine itself. The user would determine their daily dose and administer it via their preferred method.

If the closely monitored trials proved to be successful, the system could be rolled out more widely to many of those estimated 6000–8000 heavy users who consume the vast majority of meth in Aotearoa. Giving people access to a tightly controlled and affordable government supply of amphetamines or meth could have multiple benefits, they believed.

Hopefully, it would take many of the most hardcore meth users out of the black market, meaning they would no longer need to be involved with gangs or dealers and they wouldn't have to commit crime or deal P themselves in order to pay for it. The idea is that those in the programme would naturally and gradually reduce their use of meth. And giving them a guaranteed supply would free up their time from sourcing drugs and allow them to focus on things like employment and family life. If it proved to be as successful as opioid-substitution programmes have been, then you would also expect that over time fewer people would be using meth overall as you're taking the biggest users out of the illicit market.

Also, if you could remove their best customers from the market, you would be reducing the super profits delivered to the gangs and organised criminal groups that supply it. Reducing the control violent criminals have over the meth trade means reducing the crime they bring with them – less intimidation and robbery, fewer violent debt collections and bashings, in short less meth-fuelled mayhem and murder.

Unfortunately, as yet, their idea of a stimulant trial hasn't really gained any traction, just like the Law Commission's system of cautions and the mental health inquiry's call for decriminalisation.

Being tough on crime, it seems, means being dumb on drugs.

* * *

Cooking meth is simply the hottest game in town for criminal syndicates around the world right now. It's so cheap and so fast to make and yet the profits they can generate are dizzying. And with the escalation in methamphetamine production globally, only a fool would believe New Zealand is going to be able to curb its availability. If anything, it will increase.

So perhaps it's time we started listening to the experts if we're serious about trying to reduce the harm methamphetamine is undoubtedly causing in our communities. There are a whole series of intelligent, well-thought-out harm-reduction measures that have been suggested and so far ignored.

First up, we should change the law to stop the possession of drug utensils being a crime. This would stop police from prosecuting people for possessing needles, a practice which undermines the Needle Exchange programme and provides an incentive for people to discard their needles recklessly. It's a policy that needlessly places the public in danger. Removing this offence was one of the Law Commission's key recommendations nearly 15 years ago, but is still not in place.

Second, organisations like the Needle Exchange should sell utensils like straws and P pipes. And when people buy them, they can be given harm-reduction information as well. Meth pipes are frequently sold at dairies now anyway. They've delivered incredible benefits for those who inject drugs; there's no reason they can't for people who smoke and snort meth too.

Third, it's time to decriminalise the possession of meth outright, and other drugs while we're at it, and start reducing the stigma that surrounds P and acts as a barrier to people getting off it. Yes, the police are increasingly using their discretion and not prosecuting meth users, but this is inconsistent. Different police districts have wildly contrasting views when it comes to deciding whether or not it is in the public interest to prosecute someone and Māori are still way more likely to be prosecuted for possession than other groups in society.

We've seen the success of the Te Ara Oranga health-based decriminalisation approach, where problematic users are pointed towards treatment not courts. It's time for a consistent, nation-wide approach. Te Ara Oranga programmes should be rolled out across the country. For the results it delivers, it's dirt cheap. We need to start investing heavily in other rehab and treatment programmes too. At the moment there are wait times of up to a year to get into some residential facilities in Auckland. I've lost count of the number of times I've heard stories of desperate people being told there is no help available for their family member who is experiencing meth-induced psychosis. It's bleak out there.

New Zealand has been at the forefront of harm-reduction measures in the past like the Needle Exchange, so let's at least explore a stimulant trial as recommended by the Helen Clark and Drug Foundations. If it works, it could be another game changer for gradually getting people off meth and undermining the underworld's control of the drug.

The Misuse of Drugs Act 1975 is in dire need of a complete overhaul too. It's abundantly clear now that many of the drugs on it are not appropriately classified and are much safer than they were believed to be in the 1970s. The other problem with 'the Frankenstein law', as Green MP Chlöe Swarbrick coined it in Parliament, is it does almost nothing to stop people using drugs.

Of course, our other option is we don't change anything. We can accept the status quo and keep on fighting the war on P, knowing full well that we can never win.

We can continue to criminalise and stigmatise meth users, even though we know that all we're really doing is making it harder for them to stop. And perhaps we can just leave meth in the hands of the Head Hunters and Comancheros and the like, and accept the chaos and violence they bring with them.

But as we've witnessed over the last 25 years of methamphetamine use and abuse, leaving the control of a powerful and addictive drug in the hands of a country's most dangerous people is a recipe for disaster.

FURTHER READING

Chapter 1: 'We Ride on Dynamite'
New Zealand Antique and Historical Arms Gazette, Page 12, December 2020.
Pharmaceutical Society of Japan, www.pharm.or.jp/eng/psj_e.html.
Jon Bonné, ' "Go pills": A war on drugs?', *NBC News*, 13 January 2003, www.nbcnews.com/id/wbna3071789.
Greg Miller, 'Air Force May Have a Bitter Pill to Swallow in "Friendly Fire" Incident', *Los Angeles Times*, 4 January 2003, www.latimes.com/archives/la-xpm-2003-jan-04-na-pills4-story.html.

Chapter 2: Amphetamines: 'A Boon to Mankind'
'Use of "Pep" Drugs: Comment on shearer's death', *NZ Press Association*, Vol XCI, Issue 27624, 2 April 1955, p 8, https://paperspast.natlib.govt.nz/newspapers/CHP19550402.2.103.
'The properties of a drug named benzedrine as a cure for shyness …', *NZ Press Association*, Press, Vol LXXIII, Issue 22118, 14 June 1937, p 15, paperspast.natlib.govt.nz/newspapers/CHP19370614.2.102.
Redmer Yska, 'Book of the Week: Crazy, addicted, luminous Iris', *readingroom*, 10 December 2020, www.newsroom.co.nz/readingroom/book-of-the-week-crazy-harrowing-luminous-robin-hyde.
Mary Edmond-Paul, 'Robin Hyde (Iris Wilkinson), 1906–1939', *Women Prose Writers to World War I, Kōtare 2007, Special Issue — Essays in New Zealand Literary Biography Series One*, nzetc.victoria.ac.nz/tm/scholarly/tei-Whi071Kota-t1-g1-t11.html.

Chapter 4: Hungry for Business
'China Executes "Godfather of Crystal Meth" Cai Dongjia Whose Village Supplied One-third of the Country's Methamphetamine', *ABC News*, 18 January 2019, www.abc.net.au/news/2019-01-18/china-executes-godfather-of-crystal-meth/10726890.

'Myanmar Police Seize Largest Haul of Synthetic Drugs', *BBC News*, 19 May 2020, www.bbc.com/news/world-asia-52712014.

Panumate Tanraska, '15 dead after gunfight with drug smugglers near border', Bangkok Post, 9 Dec 2022, www.bangkokpost.com/thailand/general/2456279/15-dead-after-gunfight-with-drug-smugglers-near-border.

Chapter 5: Crystal Meth Academy

US Department of Justice Drug Enforcement Administration, *2020 Drug Enforcement Administration National Drug Threat Assessment (NDTA)*, March 2021, www.dea.gov/sites/default/files/2021-02/DIR-008-21%202020%20National%20Drug%20Threat%20Assessment_WEB.pdf.

Shawne K Wickham, 'From Mexican Jungles to New Hampshire Streets: Crystal Meth is Here', *New Hampshire Sunday News*, 20 February 2021, www.unionleader.com/news/crime/from-mexican-jungles-to-new-hampshire-streets-crystal-meth-is-here/article_5667cd62-42e0-58f1-acb9-b4ee300fba60.html.

Associated Press, 'Slovakia Drug Bust Yields Huge Shipment of Methamphetamines', *Yahoo! Finance*, 7 July 2020, finance.yahoo.com/news/slovakia-drug-bust-yields-huge-130559948.html.

Associated Press, 'Mexican Navy Seizes Tequila Bottles Containing Nearly 10 Tons of Liquid Meth', *The Guardian*, 25 April 2023, theguardian.com/world/2023/apr/24/mexican-navy-tequila-liquid-meth.

Chapter 6: Moral Panic

Tom Hunt, 'P Contamination Rampant and Growing in New Zealand State Homes', *Stuff*, 8 November 2015, www.stuff.co.nz/dominion-post/news/73219533/p-contamination-rampant-and-growing-in-new-zealand-state-homes.

Housing New Zealand, Press Release, 'Tribunal's Methamphetamine Rulings Send Strong Message', 24 March 2016, www.scoop.co.nz/stories/PO1603/S00411/tribunals-methamphetamine-rulings-send-strong-message.htm.

Chapter 7: Dread Pirate Roberts

UNODC Research, *In Focus: Trafficking over the Darknet – World Drug Report 2020*, www.unodc.org/documents/Focus/WDR20_Booklet_4_Darknet_web.pdf.

Chapter 8: White-collar 'Chemical Man'

Russell Brown, 'The Role Model', *Hard News*, 9 September 2003, publicaddress.net/hardnews/the-role-model.

Ministry of Health, *Drug Use in New Zealand: Key Results of the 2007/08 New Zealand Alcohol and Drug Use Survey*, 2010, www.moh.govt.nz/NoteBook/nbbooks.nsf/0/9E7BA7ADC26D9869CC2576CE00673802/$file/drug-use-in-nz-v2-jan2010.pdf.

Ministry of Health, *New Zealand Health Survey*, www.health.govt.nz/nz-health-statistics/national-collections-and-surveys/surveys/new-zealand-health-survey.

Chapter 9: 'Horrible, Horrible Man'

Vincent J Felitti, *The Origins of Addiction: Evidence from the adverse childhood experiences study*, Department of Preventive Medicine Kaiser Permanente Medical Care Program, 2004, www.nijc.org/pdfs/Subject%20Matter%20Articles/Drugs%20and%20Alc/ACE%20Study%20-%20OriginsofAddiction.pdf.

Chapter 10: Zombieland

'Marihuana "Worst Drug," says CIB Officer', *Gisborne Herald*, Press, Volume LXXVII, Issue 23211, 24 March 1950, p 5, paperspast.natlib.govt.nz/newspapers/GISH19500324.2.77.

'The Drug Menace: Scientist's grave view of expanding "dope" habit', *New Zealand Herald*, Press, Volume LXXVI, Issue 23269, 11 February 1939, p 13, paperspast.natlib.govt.nz/newspapers/NZH19390211.2.211.56.

'Editorial: Grappling with the Demon of Methamphetamine', *New Zealand Herald*, 7 May 2019, www.nzherald.co.nz/nz/editorial-grappling-with-the-demon-of-methamphetamine/7KMTVFEXGNVHNL2GN6EKTJIU4M.

Paul Charman, 'Hard-hitting Homespun Anti-meth Advertising Campaign Needed to Beat the P Scourge', *New Zealand Herald*, 16 February 2017, https://www.nzherald.co.nz/nz/hard-hitting-homespun-anti-meth-advertising-campaign-needed-to-beat-the-p-scourge/VUW34OQFC2PIKTO2UXIDSF2E4I.

University of Western Australia, Press Release, 'Success of Graphic Meth Ads Questioned by UWA Study', 10 December 2008, www.news.uwa.edu.au/archive/business-briefing/success-graphic-meth-ads-questioned-uwa-study.

D Mark Anderson and David Elsea, 'The Meth Project and Teen Meth Use: New Estimates from the National and State Youth Risk Behavior Surveys', *Health Economics*, Volume 24, Issue 12, December 2015, pp 1644–1650, onlinelibrary.wiley.com/doi/10.1002/hec.3116.

Carl L Hart, Joanne Csete and Don Habibi, *Methamphetamine: Fact vs Fiction and Lessons from the Crack Hysteria*, February 2014, www.opensocietyfoundations.org/publications/methamphetamine-dangers-exaggerated.

Lucy Harry, 'Rethinking the Relationship between Women, Crime and Economic Factors: The Case-Study of Women Sentenced to Death for Drug Trafficking in Malaysia', Laws, Volume 10, Issue 1, 2021, p 9, www.mdpi.com/2075-471X/10/1/9.

Chapter 11: Straight Shooting
Peter JW Saxton et al, 'Injecting Drug Use among Gay and Bisexual Men in New Zealand: Findings from national human immunodeficiency virus epidemiological and behavioural surveillance', *Drug and Alcohol Review*, Volume 39, Issue 4, May 2020, pp 365–374, onlinelibrary.wiley.com/doi/abs/10.1111/dar.13046.

Chapter 13: 'Havoc, Harm and Upheaval'
'Children of Cocaine', *The Washington Post*, 30 July 1989, www.washingtonpost.com/archive/opinions/1989/07/30/children-of-cocaine/41a8b4db-dee2-4906-a686-a8a5720bf52a.

Chapter 14: The Punisher
Kate Lamb, 'Philippines Secret Death Squads: Officer claims police teams behind wave of killings', *The Guardian*, 4 October 2016, www.theguardian.com/world/2016/oct/04/philippines-secret-death-squads-police-officer-teams-behind-killings.
Glee Jalea, 'Robredo Flunks Duterte Admin in Drug War, Says Less than 1 Percent Shabu Seized by Authorities in the Last Three Years', CNN Philippines, 6 January 2020, www.cnnphilippines.com/news/2020/1/6/Robredo-flunks-PH-admin-in-drug-war,-says-less-than-1-percent-shabu-seized-by-authorities-in-the-last-three-years.html.
Kate Lamb, 'Thousands Dead: the Philippine president, the death squad allegations and a brutal drugs war', *The Guardian*, 2 April 2017, www.theguardian.com/world/2017/apr/02/philippines-president-duterte-drugs-war-death-squads.
'Illegal Drugs Seized', *NZ Press Association*, Press, Volume CIX, Issue 32100, 23 September 1969, p 15, https://paperspast.natlib.govt.nz/newspapers/CHP19690923.2.125.
Peter Benchley, 'The American Scene – The Drive on Drugs: How US is counter-attacking', *Newsweek Feature Service*, Press, Volume CXI, Issue 32585, 20 April 1971, p 14, https://paperspast.natlib.govt.nz/newspapers/CHP19710420.2.108.
UNODC, Press Release, 'UNODC World Drug Report 2022 Highlights Trends on Cannabis Post-legalization, Environmental Impacts of Illicit Drugs, and

Drug Use among Women and Youth', 27 June 2022, www.unodc.org/unodc/press/releases/2022/June/unodc-world-drug-report-2022-highlights-trends-on-cannabis-post-legalization--environmental-impacts-of-illicit-drugs--and-drug-use-among-women-and-youth.html.

Global Commission on Drug Policy, Report, 'War on Drugs', June 2011, http://www.globalcommissionondrugs.org/wp-content/uploads/2017/10/GCDP_WaronDrugs_EN.pdf.

Joe Parkins Daniels, 'War on Drugs Prolonged Colombia's Decades-long Civil War, Landmark Report Finds', *The Guardian*, 29 June 2022, https://www.theguardian.com/world/2022/jun/29/war-on-drugs-prolonged-colombias-decades-long-civil-war-landmark-report-finds.

UNODC, Executive Summary, 'Survey of Territories Affected by Coca Cultivation, 2021', https://www.unodc.org/documents/crop-monitoring/Colombia/EXECUTIVE_SUMMARY_19102022.pdf.

Stefano Pozzebon, 'This Country Calls Time on the "War on Drugs"', CNN, 21 August 2022, edition.cnn.com/2022/08/21/americas/colombia-marijuana-bill-war-on-drugs-intl-cmd/index.html.

NZ Drug Foundation, 'Drugs in NZ – An Overview', www.drugfoundation.org.nz/policy-and-advocacy/drugs-in-nz-an-overview.

Craig Kapitan, 'Auckland Kidnap Case: Prison ordered for duo who helped hog-tie and torture man', *New Zealand Herald*, 16 December 2021, www.nzherald.co.nz/nz/auckland-kidnap-case-prison-ordered-for-duo-who-helped-hog-tie-and-torture-man/O2EQXRD6WSPN4XUPQOIZ5YVGEI.

Chapter 15: Frankenstein: Breaking the Cycle

Philippa Yasbek et al, 'Minimising the Harms from Methamphetamine', *The Helen Clark Foundation, NZ Drug Foundation*, 3 September 2022, helenclark.foundation/publications-and-medias/minimising-the-harms-from-methamphetamine.

ACT Government, Press Release, 'ACT to Decriminalise Small Amounts of Illicit Drugs', 9 June 2022, www.cmtedd.act.gov.au/open_government/inform/act_government_media_releases/rachel-stephen-smith-mla-media-releases/2022/act-to-decriminalise-small-amounts-of-illicit-drugs.

NSW Government, 'Landmark Investment into Alcohol and Other Drug Services as Part of the Response to the Ice Inquiry', dcj.nsw.gov.au/news-and-media/media-releases-archive/2022/landmark-investment-into-alcohol-and-other-drug-services-as-part.html.

ACKNOWLEDGEMENTS

Maybe I just got lucky, but nearly every person I approached for an interview for *Mad on Meth* agreed to talk to me. Not only were they willingly to share their often highly personal stories, but they also answered my follow-up queries again and again with good grace. It was the same with the researchers and officials who spent many hours meeting with me and answering every question I had about P. I'm indebted to all of you.

The NZ Drug Foundation's *Through the Maze: On the road to health* symposium at Parliament in 2021 was the springboard for this book, and it was there I met many of those working on the frontlines of methamphetamine – whether they be fighting it, treating it or combatting the stigma surrounding it. I'm grateful to the NZ Drug Foundation's Sarah Helm and Ben Birks Ang for facilitating many introductions that day, and for their tips and assistance since.

To my mates who helped along the way, from accessing and navigating the Dark Web, keeping me up to date with prices of meth on the street or simply chatting about interesting meth cases they'd heard about – quite a few of which made it into the book – cheers guys!

To Holly Hunter, thanks for sowing the idea for this book and talking me into it, and to Shannon Kelly and the rest of the team at HarperCollins for your assistance. My editor Jude Watson did a fantastic job helping to knock this book into shape, killing quite a few of my darlings along the way.

And finally, to my partner, Claire, for her support and encouragement and keeping our two young girls entertained while I barricaded myself in the study hour after hour, researching and writing this book – bravo!